INTERSTITIAL
ARCHAEOLOGY

WISCONSIN POETRY SERIES
Sean Bishop and Jesse Lee Kercheval, series editors
Ronald Wallace, founding series editor

INTERSTITIAL ARCHAEOLOGY

POEMS

FELICIA ZAMORA

THE UNIVERSITY OF WISCONSIN PRESS

The University of Wisconsin Press

728 State Street, Suite 443

Madison, Wisconsin 53706

uwpress.wisc.edu

Printed in the United States of America

{CIP record to come}

For Foula

We are dealing with human nature.
—JAMES BALDWIN, "James Baldwin & Nikki Giovanni Part 1"

what does it mean to be human? ~ *why do we care?*
special, special animal ~ human *is a box*

there is no poem unless   i
we can find the courage to speak
—EVIE SHOCKLEY, "what does it mean to be human?"

That silence amalgamating.
—CHRISTOPHER SOTO, "Then A Hammer // Realized Its Life Purpose"

CONTENTS

A SHARP DAWN

CLAWS WIDE IN THE MIRROR

Meditations on Lines

Water takes the path of least resistance. Any competent plumber spouts this tried & true logic. Water disobeys. Water wants what water wants. Water claims & claims. If you live in the desert long enough, you become watchful of water. Water makes up 83% of lungs; 74% of brain & heart. Tuning fork of organs. Protective. Even, our watery bones. You meet the saguaro & touch your clavicle in kindship. What you can lug around. How roots tendril inside a body. You wonder how long before the spikes & spindles evolve you.

::::

Before I was a cell, I was a whisper of a cell from another cell. A longing.

::::

Our fingers between the chain-linked fence. Our silhouettes cast into pool before our bodies. Water glistens mercury in moonlight. Our skinny limbs under layers peeling onto cement. Under the diving board, you enter me, up to knuckles. My frame squirms in the chlorine. You bring your finger to your nose. "You don't smell like a dirty taco." & I see muscles constrict along your shoulder blades, your frame pulls out of the wet.

::::

Count 499 seconds: the time for light to leave the sun & hit Earth. About eight minutes. We label this number, one; one Astronomical Unit. We define. & from our definitions, causality in abundance. The psychologist duo Dr. Susan Fiske & Dr. Shelley Taylor coined us *cognitive misers*. Our brain tendrils & pathways not unlike water, in search of facile, of ease. Why scale the redwood when the stream carries our bulbous bodies in gentle sway?

::::

Nothing about the human body suggests effortlessness.

:::::

After the plumber augers the main sewer line, he stands on the basement steps & says, "You seem like clean people," & continues his story about a slum lord who "had 15 Latinos living in a basement knee-deep in feces." He groans a chuckle. My organs flinch & my cells swell. My ears fill; I'm 15 again under water, lungs in burn & his voice muffles away as I sink further below surface.

:::::

Perhaps Fiske & Taylor got it wrong; the body made to *act in*, suggesting environment & in turn, *be acted upon*, suggesting relationship. We define to feel whole. We define to use the tongue & teeth & mandible & epiglottis to construct home in a language full of gaps; a language that, at times, despises us. Lungs & throat & air swirl & a voice emerges. Amiri Baraka said, "Context, in this instance, is most dramatically social." Our definitions fail in the linear. Think of the zigzags, the rounded curves of any context filtered through veils of haze in our hippocampus. Did we forget the circulatory systems of veins, arteries, vessels, & nerves twisting inside of us?

:::::

Maggots collect in a tiny inlet of plastic filled with water after 22 hours of rain. Half of the cream, cylindrical bodies float, still. The other half writhe & circle the dead. If design exists here, Frost, what horrid spell cast.

:::::

Light bends by itself. In 94.36 million miles, the sun's rays reach our pupils. Any physics textbook tells us light travels in a straight line. Yet we now know light bends by itself. Light travels in curves without external influence.

::::

Our walking circuitous solar systems under flesh.

::::

A lesson in windows. Corneas hold the power of refraction; the cornea bends rays through the pupil to enter us. The face: a camera & our irises: shutters. Collection built in our compositions. Ciliary muscles mold the lens' shape, bend here flatten there, to focus light & images on the retina. The rods & cones of us in photoreceptive cells. How a definition bends to desired shape. Fenestrae in the brain, in the lungs, the throat. Open the transom. Breathe.

::::

Women develop complete sets of cells. I develop from ovum living inside my mother's ovary while inside my grandma's womb. I begin immature cell from immature ovum inside a womb. I am a woman of a woman of a woman. Interior ghost in haunt.

::::

You take me to the edge of nothing. No longer palimpsest for your butchery. I wring my shins & torso & spine & forearm; collect my own fluids. Drink.

Chirality

If I cross paths with myself on the sidewalk, I'm not sure I will recognize my own face. Phone down, I consider the gravity of such interaction. Mirrors
reflect a flawed duplication, a reversal perpendicular to surface. I am
an optical effect & also the optics in creation—a geometric

consideration of my structure; how 3D of me. I think
of Mel's new printer—five hours of molten extrusion & the plastic heart
warps on one side, sunken. *It's just practice*, she smiles. *Next time,
it'll be perfect*, her fingers grip red into the camera. The human body

spores a litany of no-next-time scenarios; an *almost* statistic. In birth,
we learn how a body makes another body, how teeth fall out with promise
of other teeth, how opened flesh may be sutured, how one hair falls
& another burrows from scalp. A lacrimal bone lines each eye socket, scalelike

& thin. A face comprises fragile patchworks of collagen & calcium; I forget
the delicacy of composition; then a finger slices & I am all blood & also all metal
in saw at my own hand. Here, at the altar of the amygdala again in tuck
of hippocampi—Oh Lorde, how I am more than a casualty; how silence

succumbs & I am daughter of doubt; a limbic system born of another
limbic system. How whiteness wants to swallow my veins, pull my spine
through incisors—a meal to wipe from chin, wash hands & be done. I know
the suicide rate for every hundred thousand Latinx, 40-something women

holds at 2.6%. Scare tactic of my voice/not my voice—to unlearn the weight
of domination, I must quiet the sharp echo inside first, the voice with arms
in waive, in plead *go back in, you can't handle all these prisms*; the thing
about mirrors lies in flawed duplication. Only two enantiomorphs

ever exist: object & image. Sponges absorb nutrients from the sea floor
in their porous bodies. No brain. No nervous tissues. All survival. To learn
of self beyond the eyes: a collection of anatomical & electrical systems
in evolution in string to a skeleton. The organ wants what the organ wants

& hangs behind my ribs—object of all objects; my circulatory
energy. & in these surfaces of tissues, I discover my singularity
amid the copies of self. I consider the octopus. Octopi & squid harbor
three hearts: one systematic & two to force blood through gills. Five

aortic arches in the earthworm segment the body to pump blood. A hagfish
contains four hearts. I look at my face in the mirror. My own écorché
set against a razor white background. I reach inside my chest, fingers grip
four chambers in swell & beat; I hold the muscle up to my eyes, then glass.

Lilacs

I wet the bed until seven years old. Still of sleep abandoned to the shove of my back, *Get up, Felicia. You peed again.* I shimmied the wet shorts off my lanky frame, sniffed the edges of my T-shirt before pulling damp cotton overhead. My naked shoulders parallel to the rim of the sink, only the top of my hair visible in the mirror—what invisibility means to flesh, to a bare ass of a child waiting to be brought dry underwear & knowing only empty hands & sleeping sighs exist beyond the bathroom door.

> The Mayo Clinic says not to be alarmed for bed-wetting before age seven. Development of nighttime bladder control. Reduce bet-wetting. Treat the problem. Treat the problem. Treat the problem. Treat the problem. Did someone write *patience* next to *problem*? Did someone write *understanding* next to *problem*? Moisture alarm. Cost? Medication. Cost? Treat the problem. Roots versus symptoms. Emotional & psychological. Did someone say stress leads to a child acting differently? Nighttime wetting a symptom. Which am I?

I never told anyone what made me stop urinating in my sleep. I let my family believe in the miracle, the by-the-grace-of-god-prayers-answered or the she-just-grew-out-of-it hypotheses. Night existed in a gap of throat where silence dwells. Silence about the washer running at 2 a.m. Silence on my brother's back & sister's back turned from the light under the bathroom door. Silence on how bedtime went from 9 p.m. to 11 p.m. to midnight & my how body ached for sleep outside the night. Silence in the absence of. A family of four who sleeps in one room, washes dishes in an old shower with a hose as a faucet, doesn't utter *waterproof mattress pad* or *therapy* or *how do you feel about this, Felicia.* A family of four learns to shut three brown bodies out from the world. *Ugly. Little girls just don't do that,* grandma's blue eyes stabbed into my brown. To be born a problem was to swallow silence: medicine meant to erase. To be groomed into falsities that a word like *beauty* held space for only other words: blue, green, hazel, white, blonde, ivory, white, white. A definition depends on who speaks & who remains silent.

I never took a photo of the floor of the motel. Not checkered like other '50s-style diners at the time. No, this floor resembles tiny speckled stars on concrete coated with epoxy. Same flooring meanders into the bathroom. Night after night, my feet on the cold speckled stars. If a vault in heaven exists, would angels know me only by the patterns on the soles of my feet?

In the dream, the dream during the first night the wetting stopped, I smelled lilacs. Lilacs grew all around the motel. Wild. Amid the lilac bushes & mulberry trees & sheep's wool caught in the iron thorns of barbed wire, I dug on my haunches in wet soil behind the motel, down the hill from the clothesline, in the overgrowth of forest. Once a city dump, this forest held trinkets & objects broken & scarred—the discarded found home here. I learned to hear the voices of the damaged. Half a bone-china teacup my most prized companion. In my mind, the woman who drank tea lived in a stone cottage by a lake; the woman who drank tea tended sheep but never shaved them; the woman who drank tea dressed her bed in linens the smell of sky & storm clouds rocked her to sleep at night. This was not the dream.

Thirty years later, my sister tells me she also wet the bed until eight. *I don't remember why I stopped,* I hear the question sit in her mouth & scurry back up to her brain. Capped memories exist; thresholds in a body; survival tactics. *You were the first, Mel; the first manifests differently.* I listen for her breath. *Remember Joe, he slept-walked, peeing all over the house, yelling "fire" in Spanish?* We both search the silence for a nostalgic chuckle. Heavy silence until, *I remember.*

In the dream, the dream during the first night the wetting stopped, lips kissed my forehead while my eyes remained shut. The hand belonging to the lips took mine inside theirs, *Time to get up, Felicia.* I scooched my body off the bed & looked at the dark silhouette: a blurred face & unfamiliar frame. How can more comfort exist in the unknown? We went, hand in hand, into the bathroom. *Light?* asked the voice. *No, just hold my hand,* & I slid the right side of shorts down, then the left. Urine hit the surface of water & I began to cry. *Why?* asked the voice. Between heaves & sobs, *No, each nightmare begins with me here, thinking I'm safe, thinking it's okay,* & I buried my face in my knees. *Do you smell the lilacs, Felicia?* the voice asked. Between sobs, I sniffed. *I do. How?* The silhouette reached toward my chest & placed one shaded finger on my breastbone. *You're not my father, are you?* I asked. *Did you need me to be?* I shook my head. & the light flicked on. *Felicia.* My mom's-tired eyes went wide. *You're . . . you're on the toilet.*

Do you know the etymology of "ugly," I ask the therapist. *No, actually I don't,* she stops writing & holds her pen alert. *Comes from Old Norse, "uggligr," or dreadful, from "ugga," meaning fear.* She puts down her pad of paper, *& are you, Felicia, are you?* I look out the window as the rain turns to snow. The sun no longer visible from cover of clouds. *I smell them,* I drift. *Smell what?* I get up from the chair & move toward the door.

Ghazal Containing My Estranged Mexican Tongue

Your incisors tear flesh of the bottom lip. Tastebuds flood with iron. Jaw: a bone
unhinges from socket by fists by fists [this isn't supposed to have an arc]; jar of ribs

shakes between palms, a cocktail for the devil hides behind the vowels, round mandible
in gape to expose the blackhole of throat where conocimiento dwells in open maxilla

yet remains silent [you're fucking up foundations again] [whose foundations] in hyoid
you consider all anatomical parts rupture when pressurized; a knee breaks a sternum

crushes a nation's aortic everything [we in here, breathing after erasure]; universe in skull
synapsing across voids [lick the elbow, lick the nipple, lick the clitoris—never separate: sphenoid;

frontal; zygomatic; ethmoid; scaffolds of orbicular] orbit us, see in collection. Song in sacrum
in swivel to rhythms of nacimiento of wet & wondering cells circulating a spine

threads muscles, veins, tissues [a body a rhetorical argument form cannot unweave], costillas—
steps in a mausoleum of flesh [broken language climbs], in chest, Felicia, breaking wings from
scapulas.

Meditations on Flesh

An ulcer develops inside my lower lip in crevasse of gumline, the translucent milky gray pocks oral mucosa landscape of dark pink & I remember my flesh incubates; a home for short-lived tenets evolving a kind of *thought come to life* in the mouth— carrying the acts of membranes & cells. What haunts the body sometimes haunts from interior vantage.

::::

The ground squirrel in California chews on rattlesnake skin, spits out the paste to apply on its body—a confused rattlesnake smells its own deadly, hesitates at the familiar venom. I look in the mirror & think of all my jaws chew & spit out—I both predator & prey. How language, thistles on my tongue, in stick to flesh laid bare: pulmonary artery in expose from lick.

::::

Environment changes us. In the Alden Motel, stray cats brought fleas. My ankles swollen & torn from indentations of my own nails. Dust mites caused allergic fits: stuffy nose, runny eyes, lack of smell for weeks on end. Nudibranchs change skin coloration by changing diet. Octopi camouflage their bodies when threatened. Octopi swim fast, swim fast in open ocean.

::::

Butterfly wings contain *eyespots*, circular patterns to resemble the eyes of larger animals, to confuse & misdirect with *disruptive coloration*. The monarch butterfly uses aposematism to ward off prey. Sometimes we hide, sometimes illuminate to keep ourselves alive. The polar bear's physicality acts as prism; black skin under translucent fur reflects the sun to only appear white.

:::::

In art black contains the presence of all colors. In physics & spectrum, the opposite. To understand the human condition, we must acknowledge both theories exist simultaneously & in tandem. When my mother warned, *If you touch the monarch butterfly's wings, she can never return home; she dies*, my fingers already on the wing; too late to release; too early to understand the lie.

:::::

My left knee contains asphalt from a childhood bike accident: three kids on one dirt bike & a serious hill. My brother held my chin in his palm to the top of the hill, *Don't look down*. Only when I saw the blood, I cried. Only when I saw the blood, I felt the rip & sear of missing skin. Blue-green scar plumps & circles, itches when cold, itches long before the rest of my leg.

:::::

Biochromes absorb & reflect certain wavelengths of light; octopi harbor these microscopic pigments to change color & patterns & even opacity. To be able to see inside, become more sheer. If our skin melts transparent, if our inner workings expose, blink & glow like moon jellyfish in deep ocean, would we see each other, feel our connectivity? Or sour that too?

:::::

National Geographic tells me a rhyme for how to remember what snake patterns to be cautious of: *red on yellow kills a fellow, red on black won't hurt Jack*. The lines catch & repeat in my mind.

In summer 2020, a Starbucks barista asked the white woman to wear a required mask. She attacked him. His friends raised $100K in GoFundMe; the woman sued for half. Red on yellow.

::::

In seeing maggots on a deer carcass, my skin crawls as I watch their bodies writhe in & around each other, squirm in compost. Fly larvae, to be exact. Wikipedia says the word *maggot* doesn't exist as a technical term or in entomology. Perhaps my reaction stems from misunderstanding. Perhaps the heap of bodies clangs a bell, reminds me of love; a closeness gone missing.

Learned Intimacy

The curvature of a shoulder: place where flesh gathers to flesh. Slope of ear lightly suctions. Your eyes roll under REM-induced drifting. Incantations spell from your lips, parted, a fissure in my universe. I bow my hips out from your leg, slide my hand beneath the lace & begin to masturbate. How the word *passionate* dilutes in comparison to my index finger & wisp of your breath hinting the scent of milky dandelion sap; I chuckle in gasps. On haunches, you held the delicate head between forefinger & thumb, *It's latex, you know.* I stood above you imbibing your frame. *Dandelion sap.* I hold my moan at the back of my throat. Exhale the word *l-ay-t-ex*, in long syllabic filaments. Arch my spine up to a rhythm of my own making. I first found my clitoris at the edge of a couch arm— mons pubis applying pressure into fabric until the sturdy of wood found, then down to prepuce, until almost sting. My pelvis worked the curve while eyeing for my mother washing dishes around the corner. Even at six, I knew the relief an organism gives the body. Wanting leaves traces. & I knew the world wanted to keep me wanting. I learned to take my own breath away. I learned to lean into the arm of the couch while keeping eyes in lookout. The thought of my head thrown back, eyes clutched, veins pulsating heat, reflected in my mother's widened eyes haunted me. & yet wanting leaves traces so I evolved the efficiency of cumming. I think of all that women must withhold. I think of my mother's silhouette sleeping in her car before the sun came up; how she traded bruises for factory work & three brown kids & whispers from pews; the one-body indent in the mattress for forty years; how hunger dwells in our cells, our genetics. I think had she just walked around the corner, seen me, she'd think, *Yes, this is my daughter. My lineage.* My chest deflates, fingers stop & my clitoris burns. I roll away from your chest, your sleep, your not knowing. Quiet. & I watch an episode of Agatha Christie's *Poirot.* I think of how Christie made arsenic the woman's choice for poisoning & poisoning the woman's choice for murder; how low levels of arsenic found in soil, water, air—almost untraceable. In elements, it's all about exposure, amounts. I imagine the atomic number 33. I imagine the Earth's crust. My palms gently glide over my arms, wrists, thorax. I imagine my mother, recording reruns of *Gilligan's Island*, forearms invisible under the afghan over her midsection, beads forming on her brow.

Abecedarian for My Estranged Mexican Tongue

Antecedent bellows   cállate chica   deciduous (descendant) erasure

         fantasized   gutturals

       homage injury justifies killing language   la llaga

mandible naturalized (neutralized)   ñoñería obliterate phonetics

         queres recitation (recuerdo)   arreglas skull

trachea & uvula vicissitudes   welkin xyloid, yields   zero (zeniths).

Exhume

You want the horror story in your palate, a miniature set of ribs in the mouth, to crack. Another bare-hearted beginning. The eggs in the refrigerator were never meant to hatch. We design certain delicacies for a hot skillet. If you're not the flame & not the skillet. A mnemonic device exists for your flame-to-skillet riddle & yet your tongue rolls back; you swallow papillae-covered muscle. Empty games in empty cavities. You once played hide-&-seek in a Victorian house. Cramming your small body far back into a pantry crease, your head bumps & papers tumble from behind tin canisters. Photographs & tracings of vulvas agape between thighs, veins of a cock like an ariel map, bruised wrists & buttocks, blood in pubic hair barely sprouted. Palm on a burner. Palm on a burner too slow before flesh sears. Her name swings on your epiglottis. You want to understand horror. How a neighbor slaps his child, then that child slaps another boy calling him *dirty spic*, then that boy grows sleepwalking to his own screams of *Fuego! Fuego!* into the mirror while his sisters watch him sweat, then that boy's sister grows up to fuck a boy in a basement next to pickle jars & muzzle loaders after he whispers *The previous owner hanged himself from that rafter* & you remember slatted sun through the basement window—thinking, *Do my labia resemble a mouth's O before scream?* You don't forget your brother's screams or that rafter or her name in your throat—places where secrets keep. A secret nestles between lungs, a double-layered membrane hides the throbbing. Your mouth says *Pericardium* with ease. Your mouth says *Phantasmagoria* with ease. Words become secrets when you hold your breath. A secret tangles an organ in knots until airways block. Hold your breath. When you close your eyes: the Victorian house. Hold your breath. When you close your eyes: her name. Hold your breath. You know the family's surname. Hold your breath. How you transpose *Uvula* & *Vulva* yet your mind understands anatomic locations. Hold your breath. You think of incisors & canines chewing insides of cheeks raw. Hold your breath. You think of her name. *Often* swells in your amygdala. You think of her name right now, tongue sliding down your esophagus.

Meditations on Ghosts

I believed, once, in Ouija boards, of standing in front of my own reflection mouthing *Bloody* _____, *Bloody* _____, *Bloody* _____—& how still I hesitate because I know words transfigure tongues as easily as brain, transfigure to spells cast without my consent—in anticipation of monsters who don't resemble my cheek bones, my clavicle, my left ear lobe slightly tipping forward, who don't live in motel rooms—someone says *Bates* & I wish myself Hitchcock not Perkins—in *Number 3*: a counting of three brown kids drawn inside a blueprint, blueprint of a 1950s motel drawn with charcoal so the pencil may turn at any moment to eraser. I believed, once, in a spirit here, then broken. I name this in my lungs with breath in heaves in singed burn rhyming my name already in astral plane.

::::

Gloria, I'm scared too. A mouth open. A mouth closed. This page a mouth: chewing corners raw, grinding down molars to indistinguishable rubble & with jaws, I sift, build voice from chalky dust.

::::

Ohio fog brings the scent of acorn & wet soil. Behind the Alden Motel, I lift the same acorn, 623 miles away, 32 years in the past. We pretend to know time. Nothing more elusive than imprint of an imprint of compounding seconds, minutes, hours metabolizing in flesh. I grow age in bones as thistle: the weed wanting garden.

::::

Buzz. Grandpa called him Buzz. So we called him Buzz. A singular name. Name in resistance to memory. Buzz, a sound reverberating tongue & molars & mandible. The Alden Motel's Madonna—our Prince among the rows & rows of ears, fields of ears: corn & flesh alike. *Don't ask questions.* Grandpa's words seeded in hearts & lungs, yet our brains persisted. Our minds in constant *disobey* back then. During the 1992 presidential election, the first time I saw Ross Perot on TV, I said, *That man looks like Buzz.* Smallness held in limits of gravel, tree lines, train tracks, sheep bleats by the motel—before shear.

::::

Finch's carcass flattens grass. Left wing severed down to nub. Right wing expands—coverts & tertials in full spread, before. Acknowledgment of another type of flight.

::::

Gloria, I itch at borders; the deep scrape before puss erupts in fountain from the body & my own flesh under my nails, thinking this too another type of relocation. The migration inside me itches to bone. *Stayed too long?* the voice in marrow wonders. *Too long where?* my ventricles ask, in search of burrow, of dirt of the dirt where my cells root & I taste language withheld from my tongue; how the discomfort of contradictions aches. How body. Possession of me. I commune with my own nakedness. I am a mouth. A mouth speaking unsettling things.

::::

Humus lends the soil fertility. Decompose me under a Strawberry Moon, when my larynx refuses respiration & phonation, a gift handed back to plants & animals that lay beside in dirt.

::::

Buzz died in Number 8. Office phone ringing off the hook. *I had a dream, Felicia.* Mel called from her dorm. *Is Buzz okay?* Mel knew before my mom knocking, before the spare key, before we found his body. She knew, the way a spirit touches your shoulder & says, *Don't cry* & you cry nonetheless.

::::

Grandpa Bernard ate liver and pickled pigs' feet. Grandpa Bernard's square face resembled the old man from *Up*. I cry intermittently throughout that movie. Every. Time. Grandpa Bernard raised fists. Grandpa Bernard called me *faker* just before my appendix burst. Grandpa Bernard said, *Don't throw away that box, that's a good box.*

Remnants from the '30s, shadows of *enough*.
Variations of depression. Grandpa Bernard held
my wrists until they bruised. Grandpa Bernard
spit the words *spic* & *dirty* & *beaner* at my brown face
over & over. I read Traumatology is a branch of
medicine. Vocabulary of wounds—he trained me
in the etymology & phonology of ache.

::::

What exists in the gaps: wanting wanting.

::::

In tempered light, clouds constrict the morning
walk after fireworks—bloody paw prints, 27
on concrete; a wound gone missing.

::::

Always talking about race. Of dandelion whose
flower eventually turns to seed head, to love of
the sickening cycle & to decimation. Language's
hidden spots, sunken. To resist, I move my
elbow, twist around my ankle, raise & lower my
shoulder blades: a dissecting of what motion
means to a body with inertia, with momentum in
lug after lug—all before a pulmonary quiet.

::::

In his last years, Grandpa Bernard barely washed.
His atrophied leg, a slender twig from once girthy
log & lower jaw partially removed: an orange-

sized tumor—reminders of an earlier version of person in his bones. Half-grown stubble weeds from his chin & a lingering odor of skin withheld too long from water & soap & musty sting of ripe pubic hair. Yesterday, out on my walk, I inhaled the same stench, aroma wafting from my flesh, hair follicles, sweat glands. What else does my body harbor in the lineage of sour?

::::

Gloria, I want to empty. Yet. The damn game where I stand in front of the mirror. I want saliva of naming, to wet my howl on something other than grief. I dig. I dig. I dig. I dig. I dig. I dig. I dig. In the unearthing, I find.

::::

I hid a mouse behind the carport. I scooped weight of a small, bulbous thing onto cardboard & hid behind the carport. I sat with the inanimate form of the mouse until dusk. My forehead in my hands, I wanted to believe we prayed together, prayer for release. Only one of us held the log. One of us did what he told us to do. I understood haunting that evening, what might possess.

::::

Gloria, I too grope for words. My dust-devil heart. All this time, I chase my own ribs, each stair of bone, a climb. I chase my own innards. I am not alone.

::::

Gloria, my expectations continue to condition me: when he told me, *You'll amount to nothing*, your words, only just written, unread by my five-year-old eyes, found their way into my bloodstream. Chicana daughter of doubt—I label myself now. I *am* a dangerous beast. I bring discomfort in shaking the white gaze brown, in my skin, in mind thinking, in desires manifesting. I spread claws wide in the mirror. Lick fangs. *Rar Rar Rar.*

INSCRIBING ANEW

Sonnets to Break the Crown of Invisibility

I

Here, I saved this for you, she pushes the white book
with an outline of a Gerber-baby-esque face embossed
in gold into my hands. *Your baby book*, she smiles
with teeth exposed. She only smiles with teeth
for family. In photos, only pursed lips, upturned. I
cock my head, being 33 years old & feeling a weight
from a record of myself I never knew existed. Open
the snapping binding to the smell of stale musk. In the flip,
not a snip of hair, fingerprint, photo in sepia-ed '70s or '80s
squares & a blank line after, *This book belongs to*: quiet of white
space, not mine to inhabit: a thought of a thought
never beyond a spark in her cerebellum, a smudge-
less trace of zero ink on a single page, in all 52 pages—
empty. My body a ghost of an outline, reverberates.

‖
My body a ghost of an outline, behind empty glass,
reverberates. I watch two white women in spandex stand
in my lawn. A young boy flips a ball in his hands, mouths
mother & then *fucker*, sailing the ball into my window. Two
women continue to talk. I open my door, *Hey, can I*
help you? falls from my jaws, breath to a weathered dandelion
head, *I thought I heard something* (& my mind questions *neighborly*
& *whiteness* in one synaptic fire) *hit my window.* One white mother
looks me up & down. *No*, she squints with her eyes, turns
her head, a swivel to wipe my form. Trampoline hinges
spring & spring from the neighbor's yard—screams
of children on woven polypropylene canvas, suspended
dovelike above the darkness of matt: a lamb's unknown
bleat before shear of season or before slaughter to eat.

|||

Shears of season, bleats before slaughter eat
the sky above Cavan Town. Your forearms over railing
moist air in your lungs. You left the desert to whittle
your mind from aorta back to cranium. To divert
the narrative; a narrative burning in your guts. In this lough,
stories build inside you. The thing about the Danish folktale
is the emperor *wants* to be duped—*wants* to believe in a type
of specialness—to walk his bare cock 'n' balls into a crowd
of hungry mouths to say, *I choose to be barren. Go fuck your
emaciated bodies I created*, the type of specialness rival
to zebra mussels filtering & storing polychlorinated biphenyl
& other contaminants to feed back to birds & fish that feast
on their molluscan foot. This toxic story—specialness
astray in mind, skin color, blood, in whose bare ass get exposed.

||||

Mind astray in whose skin color, whose blood gets exposed
to bare the violence of shootings. A nation sits on its ass
on gun control—eight more people murdered in Indianapolis
just weeks after the shooting at a Boulder King Soopers
just a week after massacres at three spas in Atlanta—a nation
sits on its ass, ignores the crowds filling Logan Square Park
with cries for Adam Toledo, cries for justice for all Black
and Brown people killed at the hands of police. A nation sits
laminating an open wound, vulnus sclopetarium—anatomic
site of injury—repeats in stagnation. Repeats in stagnation.
Repeats in stagnation. Stagnation. Stagnation. Anatomic site.
In AD 79, Vesuvius erupted volcanic avalanches, baked
humans to death. Cranial cavity fragments show a brain
turned to glass. 24 million minds on fire—a sharp dawn rises.

||||

What turns to glass? 24 million+ on fire—sharpness rises,
dawning a suspension of blast from a lightning bolt striking
sand. Flashes versus the strike: the way 270,000 miles per hour
hits a beach of quartz or silica & temperatures shoot to 180
degrees Celsius; a fusing, a becoming fulgurite. Petrified
lightning: hollow, glass-lined tubes, encased in sand. Calcified
snake in stretch of flashes & heat, reaching out of the dunes
to pray to the lightning, *Take me with you. Don't forget me here
inside my body, I am you.* How we cannot see the glass in layer
below granular chrysalis, unless we rip apart the body, dermis
in flay, to see the bones of the thing. How we destroy in all
this mining, curiosity, this digging for the lightning, or what
the lightning creates, only to find the ghost of pressure & fire
in wake of what our eyes & hands were never meant to capture.

||||||

In wake to what my eyes & hands were never meant to capture
as my legs pause, my torso accordions to my haunches to watch
the ants swarm the earthworm's carcass, stretch the small, bristled
setae further & further out onto concrete. How the worm's body
in devour mimics the move & burrow from life. The annuli, 100–
150 ring segments in fuse with mouth in lead, appear almost
indistinguishable under shadows & ant thoraxes. Earthworms
breathe through skin. Which annuli breathed last? Did the cerebral
ganglion know each ring in collapse? I rub my ribcage, just below
my left clavicle. With five aortic arches, I know the worm harbors
organs for feast in a tube-inside-tube structure. Phylum Annelids
in Latin means "little rings." In synapses, my brain echoes a tune
little rings, little rings in repeat at the back of my throat, in dissolve
with each lip parting, in a type of dirge—with my tongue, the pyre.

||||||

Each lip parts, in a type of dirge—with my tongue, the pyre
blowing breath—steam in collect behind thoracic cage, pulmonary
ventilation turns to soot. Always this anatomy of breathing
& how we always one part inspiration & one part expiration—
give & take of us: a body made to disintegrate. Pay attention
to any foundation to understand fault lines, gaps, a crack
in drywall—how any new contractor tells you, *Let the house
settle first, before painting the walls.* Do they not know to paint now
as the wall may only be the wall in this moment? Do they not
know a well-cared-for thing, too, crumbles? Darwin's Arch collapses
into the Pacific Ocean today. Natural erosion. Does the archipelago
feel the arch's absence? Our memories burn a silhouette 141 feet
high, 230 feet long, 75 feet wide in suspension above ocean. Do we
sound a bell of mourning? Bell of celebration? Feel our vestiges tingle.

||||||||

Sound a bell to morning's rise. Bell of celebration to feel our vestiges
tingle, O organs of haunt, still inside or removed from flesh. Delicious
reminders of lineage, of the oceanic wet inside the wet of our
724 trillion cells. *The Atlantic* article speaks of how the sea cucumber's
anus serves as makeshift mouth & digestive waste hole & pearlfish
refuge & faux lung & weapon—invertebrate Echinodermata in leathery
skin. The cucumber hurls a web of internal organs at predators to ensnare.
Cucumber breaks down detritus, recycles nutrients for other bacteria
to continue degradation. O being of function, being thought so simple
so misunderstood, I sound a bell to your endoskeleton, to connective tissues
joining ossicles—to armors we must all carry inside—to hold the weight
of our own frame, to ever evolution. My skeleton under flesh shakes hips;
my skeleton under flesh jumps Double Dutch; my skeleton under flesh bows.
Trailblazer teach us: vessel transfiguration; never just one being, always plural.

||||||||||

Trailblazers, teach us: vessel transfiguration; never just one synapse, always
plural inside a sequence of continuation. Pi, each one of us. Fibonaccies
spiraling into design after design of Romanesque broccoli steeples & disc
florets of sunflower heads; the absurdity in replication, the comfort in
expansion; how no ratio exists in the golden ratio. The irrational number
of us, where we slide into infinity, unable to chart to pinpoint exactness
of cognition, of a mind in reel. Dissect the floret down: pollen, stigma,
style, anther, corolla, ovule, ovary. Being both sums & wholes & somas
& holes. The brain a command center made of 60% fat, 40% water
& proteins & carbohydrates & salt. Equation your brain & you get
inanimate matter not adding up. Gray matter processes & interprets us
while white matter transmits throughout the nervous system: highways
of the chemical; highways of the electrical. Neuron trailblazers carve
thoughts in cerebrum, brainstem, cerebellum: our unsolvable circuit boards.

||||||||||

Thoughts in cerebrum, brainstem, cerebellum: our unsolvable circuit boards
blink behind, blink beyond. In 1993, my brother disappeared for three days.
S** dumped him; brown & fluent in Spanish & my brother felt less alone
in sharing his characteristics with S**; & tangentially, I felt less alone, even
while struggling through Spanish I with the white teacher rolling her *r*'s
faster than me, conjugating hablar to hablas better than me, more Mexican
than me, grinning behind her lipstick-smeared incisors. Specter of my brother's
tongue awarding me A after mediocre A. A brown body always before me; I
admit, a white one too. Cells: carriers of the body's hereditary material. I use
estranged next to *culture* in sentences now; excuses for a mouth, unwilling
bovine who never learns to chew her own cud. Calling myself *animal* &
salivating in the possibility of what I may bring back up from the stomach
to swallow again. My brother left. His chest a ruckus we both knew needed
taming in Alden. He disappeared & I thought, *Goddamn, Joe. Take me with you.*

|||||||||||

Taming in Alden meant a disappearing of thought. *Goddamn, Joe. Take me with you
& P****.* I begged to go with them. Begged. P****, the kid who called Joe
& me *taco fuckers* & slapped Joe in the face repeating *beaner beaner beaner* until the red
wore off after hours not minutes, & I begged to go with them. A mind sabotages
from the interior when synapses raise hairs where the skull curves toward the spine
& your amygdala warns before your thinking: *flee flee flee flee flee.* The little impulses
we ignore due to learned interpretations of impoliteness, or even, indiscernible
acts. In the basement, after burnt pizza & dick jokes & Frogger, P****'s brother
raised a two-by-four. In the basement, P****'s brother cracked a septum. In
the basement, *Shut up you little cunt*, & breath held. In the basement, blood
& the smell of half-lit kerosine lamps & mildewing towels. Then, *Get the fuck
out.* We left P**** in his own snot & piss & blood. We left P**** in the basement
at hands larger than his own & ran the seven blocks back to the Alden Motel. In
weeks following, my jaws refused to want outside of shut; a hinge knowing.

||||||||||||

Weak follows my jaws, a refusal to want outside of shut; a hinge knowing
the damage of open: to let in or let out. How the humpback whale's mouth
expands up to 10 feet, yet the throat widens only 15 inches in diameter—how
my esophagus holds memories: in constriction, in gasps. Whale's body expels
& breathes air as mammal. Evelyn Green owned the sheep pasture adjacent
to the Alden Motel. Evelyn Grimes, my grandmother, brought her goulash
& ham sandwiches with mustard on dinner rolls. Both Evelyns shared
a pastoral thinking of living in Iowa in the 1980s. Both Evelyns rolled
their short gray hair in curlers each night, wore costume pearls, & polyester
pants in summer. From the necks of both Evelyns swung golden crosses
with the outline of Jesus in crucifixion linens embossed. Evelyn Green's piano
sat in the parlor just before the back sunroom. Grandma sent me to deliver
leftover church lilies. *Would you teach me to play?* I asked Evelyn Green. *Oh
dear, don't touch. Children like you become ditch diggers.* Humpback, unable to surface.

||||||||||||

Dear, don't touch. Children like you become ditch diggers. I am the humpback, unable to surface inside my whale heart, my whale brain. Evelyn Green's words radiate under my epidermis even after 30 years. I remember the whale's aorta measures over nine inches, yet the heart only consists of 1% body weight. Water supports the weight of whales. Water helps construct the shape of whales we know. How an environment molds the body. Evelyn Green's words remind me, whales' ears, the only mammalian ears to adapt fully underwater, hold the broadest acoustic range of any mammal. In my dive, in my sink, the surface remains above—a spell cast to tempt bones back out of the depths—when I stay in the wet, as the wet, when I linger my pulsed calls, clicks & whistles permeate the waters, across 321 cubic million miles of ocean to reach the ears of other whales, whales who understand a body living half in air & half in water will always be misinterpreted, misrepresented. To examine a whale out of water means to ignore plurality in the mechanisms of anatomy. To examine a whale under water means no examination exists, only witness to a body in motion, a body alive. Water inside us echoes. Environment sculpts us & we sculpt environment. How human of our animality.

Environment echoes us, sculpts us & we sculpt environment. Concepts of human & animality carve deep wounds of racist hierarchy & antiblackness from western humanism thinking. Zakiyyah Iman Jackson argues black matter as nonrepresentability "holds the potential to transform the terms of reality and feeling, therefore rewriting the conditions of possibility of the empirical." Newton invokes the law of inertia. Newton explains Kepler's law. Newton establishes the science of gravitation: attractive force connecting all bodies with mass. All bodies. All bodies. All bodies? I lick iron from the corners of my mouth. The Birwood Wall in northwest Detroit, 6' high, 12" thick, erected behind Margaret Watson's house in 1941: brick & mortar manifestation of segregation, alive & still damaging; a thinking that *human*, a term never meant for us, the colonized, the enslaved Brown & Black people, only *beast, beast, beast & we left with a language not not not not not not not* a mantra of being, of those who no longer wish the "humanist prize," who seek existences with our bodies, safe inside. Nietzsche, I no longer accept concepts as gifts. Ocean tides & centrifugal forces existed before the words *moon & Earth*. Imagine us, inscribing anew.

Tides & centrifugal forces existed before the words *moon* & *Earth*. Imagine us, inscribing new divinations of being. In mathematics, *i* signifies the imaginary unit: imaginary number: solution to the quadratic equation $x^2 + 1 = 0$, or square root of negative one. *i* holds no property, no real number yet real in thinking; *i* extends the real numbers, makes them complex numbers by using addition & multiplication. I make my I an *i*. I make my *i*, I make my eye an *i*. I make my *i* an eye. I am both +i & -i on the Cartesian plane, steeped in a vertical axis of above & below in all my dimensions. My cerebrum extends the conversation in the all-white, all-male boardroom. My collar bone extends the playground from kickball court to boxing ring. My cochlea extends his jaw hesitant in silence before the question *Why did God give Mexicans noses?* His idea of "a joke." My salivary glands & ducts spit out all the "jokes"; how only tiny slivers, close to the surface, work their way out when skin sheds. How you want to believe the body pushes out deep splinters, ingrown & yet the infection persists. All those fucking jokes. My *i*/eye transforms the equation: asks to see this breath mixing with air, these lungs filling, this chest cracking & throbbing, these labia quavering, this cerebral cortex contemplating me & us—*i* a force of matter extends a reckoning.

LEAVING HALVES

Poem about Human Habits of Consumption
That Begins with Contemplating the Walnut in My Yard

Hidden in the lawn at my foot: a black walnut, halved,
a vomer bone nestled in skull, heart-shaped & snout-
like. Insides reveal holes—empty sockets with eyes
removed; kernels once held in curvature of space.
A glistening sliver catches my vision; I turn casing
between fingers, search an exterior for a slit of light
to see. Rain holds in your tiny body—how you always
hold rain from root to fruit—a miniature mirror to hold
the world in shards. Your bulbous green husk, long
removed, your wooded carriage, pried. Who parted
your shell, in wedge & tear? How hunger claws
first from a belly. What we expose in our wanting.
Who suckled from you once? Who suckles from you
now? A *who who who* repeats, conjures a scene in mind
as if we were not talking plants influencing other plants,
as if we were not talking animal, as animal. How *crave*
builds first below a ribcage, within an artery, just below
dermis. We know feathers & talons transport—we bird
beaks *peck peck peck*; we *Sciuridae*; we language outside
our mouths; we tree-squirrel-milk-teeth in wait
to be reborn incisors; we foragers the lot—turkeys,
racoons, bears in our guts, talking—we do talk—
how mammalian of us in our scuttle of forests, pastures,
caverns, buttes, waterways, airwaves, prying open &
dismantling in our gait. We know of defenses, of our
roots evolving: a sour kind of love. We allelopathic
plants; we emit a toxicity, making others susceptible: pines,
birch trees, azaleas, nightshades. Influence bound & we
want to make this all biological; how the false superiority
of our cells continues to wound; we influencers of

germination, reproduction, growth, survival of
another. We sunflowers, saying the word *sunflower*,
a smirk in our tallness, our big heads, our must-be-
unique beauty—in our inhabitations, in the space of taking,
in the space of taking space, we groan & chomp, leaving halves.

To Haunt Air: In Consideration of Longing, the Potoo, Desire, Gallstones, & What We Remain Still For

maaawwwwmmm. Silence. *maaawwwwmmm.* Silence. *maaawwwwmmm* echoes
in your headphones. You listen to the calls, how the plumed frame opens
& caws out deep repetitions, *aww*-filled melancholy to make the night thick
with grief. You cock your head. Your head not in the Amazon Basin, not
the Caribbean, not anywhere in South America. Your body in Ohio,
the night before the Doppler radar bounces microwave signals off
objects in the distance; before velocity data casts spells & the sky quilts
the landscape in cold white. When you feel the heaviness of such whiteness
you turn to myth. You turn your chin to the moon, ripe yellowness replicates
in the sclera of the Potoo. Magic eyes. Upper eyelids slice with small folds
to sense movement even when closed—the sense of seeing before seeing:
your knee in ache before frost; blood, a slow drip in nasal passage before
flake; burn along scapulae long before the doctor uttered *gallstones*, before
incisions to suck out the small pouch in tuck below the liver: how a seedpod
grows, appendage of another seedpod. A gallbladder: remnants of evolution
turned another direction; what we forget inside us; what makes us incomplete
also makes us complete. In Ecuadorian lore, a man and a woman lose
each other in lianas in the rainforest. Aóho turns into a bird; her husband,
the moon. The Shuar people say she wails *aishirú, aishirú,* or *my husband, my*
husband. Are we not unlike Aóho, the Potoo, crying into darkness for others
to feel what we feel? Urutaú, *ghost bird.* How the Potoo yearns for the glow
of another & itself harbors the glow; glow a gift of vision. Desire inhabits
us, because our cells born from desire. Insectivore, Potoo's mouth opens
similar to a humpback whale's, to scoop in moths, termites, beetles. In perch,
in perfect stillness, feathers melt into bark through daylight. What we remain
still for & bellow out for as the day dissolves. Another story of children
abandoned by parents with no food to provide. They too become Potoos.
Eternal *maaawwwwmmm* flows from their lungs—both lament & howl, *why*
to a mother's turned back. *maaawwwwmmm* hangs, sheer linens on moon beams,

the ghost of the ghost in moan after mournful moan—you think of vaccines;
you think of phases sanctioned by the state; you think of Pfizer-BioNTech
& Moderna. You wonder how you haunt the air as dusk hugs the sun
into horizon's belly—with large swooping wings, motioning, *Come in, come in.*

Tautology of Phrases, Tautology of Mathematical Logic in a Time of Climate Crisis

Consider acts in repeat. A litany of repetitions: a flood of statistics
about floods, rising tides, melting icebergs, fires, disintegrating

tropical forests, hurricanes, disappearing polar bears—*one
lone cub slides down the snowy terrain as the mother plods*

on with the other cub at her heels—we want to feel moved
by all this movement & yet the aggregating sea anemone

at risk in the warming waters. The coral. The coral reefs
make up 1% of the Earth's surface yet harbor 25%

of all ocean species. The Great Barrier Reef bleaches
again, 1,500 miles of coral turning white due to high ocean

temperatures: the world's oceans absorb 93% of heat
trapped in atmosphere by greenhouse gases. We want

to love the coral: the tiny polyps forming colorful colonies,
building limestone reefs, collecting algae to convert sunlight

into food. We want to see ourselves in the coral: lulled
into tide streams, gorging growth, & then—the heat. In lies

the trickery of language: *victim* versus *perpetrator*. We create
the heat. We bleach the coral. We emit the gases then say

Let's figure out how to measure, always our incorrectness in
incorrect order. Our human acts acting, heating, poisoning,

burning surfaces in our wake. In the Bloomberg article,
Kim Stanley Robinson makes us think about carbon-

negative, densification, verticalization. Kim Stanley Robinson
reminds us only 3% of wild animal biomass still exists; the other 97%

consists of humans & human-raised animals for food—our
food. Our food. Our. Feed us. Our food. Our. Our. Feed.

Feed. Our. Do we tire of hearing our own demands decimate
the Earth? Kim Stanley Robinson tells us the UN counts 4.3

billion earthly city dwellers, draws images of parks suspended
at skyscraper levels, tells us cities may be keys to saving civilization.

We civilization saving civilization. We want to listen. Work
of industrialization now turns upside down. This imaginative

work takes discipline—& we spoiled brats unable to see through
our seas of manufacturing plants, fracking drills, carbon dioxide

& methane emissions, poisoned lakes, gasoline wars, dried-up
aquifers. We want to hope. We turn our chins up to the night, turn

to the vastness with prayers as empty as the Boötes Void; our cell-phone
satellites blot out the stars. No Hollywood ending rolls here. No one

saves the Earth from us but us. We want to believe a footprint
transforms by recycling plastic yogurt containers, one by one, container

by container, reusing trash bags, riding our bikes to work. We search
websites to research our home's footprint in equations. Electricity:

use (kWh/yr) * EF (kg CO_2e/kWh) = emissions (kg CO_2e/yr) &
Natural Gas: *use (therms/yr) * EF (kg CO_2e/therms) = emissions*

(kg CO_2e/yr). We faulty in our theorems. We ask the wrong
questions. We want to ignore facts. Our economic sectors, our

businesses-as-usual burn a path for rampant greenhouse emissions.
Burning of natural gas, oil, & coal for electricity & heat create

the largest source of global greenhouse gases at 25%, followed
by 24% from agriculture in cultivation of livestock & crops

& deforestation, then 21% of industry involved in burning fossil
fuels. We add & we add. We want to think ourselves math-

e-ma[t/g]icians. Rules & rule makers. & a false division creeps
into our calculations, our foundations fracturing beneath us: our

inability to balance an equation of land ethics with a climate
shifting by our industrialization, our laws, our hands, our decisions,

our development, our patterns. We want to believe the stars still
exist beyond the satellites. We want to believe the bleached coral's

colors return. We want to believe the recycled labels of 5 & 6
don't end up in dead Pacific loggerhead sea turtles' stomachs.

We want to believe in fantasy, of an ozone healing. We must first
believe in language, in the mantra of *we caused this*. We must first

believe the logic—of species dying, wetlands diminishing, heat
rising, coastal erosions—as fact. We must then believe in large

systemic changes—how at least five ice ages & 12 epochs
of glacial expansion occurred in the past million years—how

an economy won't matter if we usher in another ice age—
in structures restructuring, in imagination of how humans create

their way in & their way out: a global effort for a global climate
crisis. We must be willing to place the sea anemone within our

vote, place the coral's value before broken policies, go beyond
belief to action—then repeat for necessity, repeat for our survival.

Taut   **Logic**

      of   **Crisis (Part)**

A litany   of statistics

melting

terrain

movement &

warming waters

Earth's surface

temperatures

collecting

lies

perpetrator We create

gases

poisoning

animals

Our

Feed

draws

civilization

upside down

see

prayers

here   one

earth   believe

one

home

in

facts Our

rampant greenhouse emissions

global

industry

makers &   false
foundations

shifting   laws

We
We

We

We

caused

species dying
fact

changes

an economy

of

global   climate

crisis   within our

vote

act   repeat   repeat

Errata

Just A through A.1.8. *Is this all we can handle?* Erratum.
Method: for us/*not for us*. Language: for us/*not for us*.

A. ~~The~~ Current State ~~of the Climate Since AR5, improvements in observationally based estimates and information from paleoclimate archives provide a comprehensive view of each component of the climate system and its changes to date. New climate model simulations, new analyses, and methods combining multiple lines of evidence lead to improved understanding of~~ human influence ~~on a wider range~~ of climate ~~variables, including weather and climate~~ extremes. ~~The time periods considered throughout this Section depend upon the availability of observational products, paleoclimate archives and peer-reviewed studies.~~

How we must label, must control. Erratum. Begin
in language. Erratum. *Begin in senses. Brine in the wave as wave.*

A.1 ~~It is~~ unequivocal ~~that human influence has warmed the~~ atmosphere, ocean and land. ~~Widespread and rapid~~ changes ~~in the atmosphere, ocean, cryosphere and biosphere have occurred. {2.2, 2.3, Cross-Chapter Box 2.3, 3.3, 3.4, 3.5, 3.6, 3.8, 5.2, 5.3, 6.4, 7.3, 8.3, 9.2, 9.3, 9.5, 9.6, Cross-Chapter Box 9.1} (Figure SPM.1, Figure SPM.2)~~

Lode stone in throat; to read & be exhausted in entry. *Persist.*

How we study study study. Us us us. How we document, document,
document. Us us us. Erratum? Depends who's listening. *We in the gaps—agape. What we know got us here.* Let us get to the guts of us.

A.1.1 ~~Observed~~ increases ~~in well-mixed~~ greenhouse gas ~~(GHG) concentrations since around 1750 are unequivocally caused by human activities. Since 2011 (measurements reported in AR5), concentrations have continued to increase in the atmosphere, reaching annual averages of 410 ppm for~~ carbon dioxide (CO_2), ~~1866 ppb for~~ methane (CH_4), ~~and 332 ppb for~~ nitrous oxide (N_2O) in ~~2019.~~ Land and ocean ~~have taken up a~~

~~near-constant proportion (globally about 56% per year) of~~ CO_2 ~~emissions from human activities over the past six decades, with regional differences (high confidence).[7] {2.2, 5.2, 7.3, TS.2.2, Box TS.5}~~

Breathe. *We can't.* Breathe. *We can't.* Breathe. *We can't.* Breathe. *We can't.* Breathe. *We can't.* Breathe. *We can't.* Breathe. *We can't.* Breathe. *You're not listening.* Erratum.

A.1.2 ~~Each of the last four decades has been successively warmer than any decade that preceded it since 1850.~~ Global surface temperature ~~in the first two decades of the 21st century (2001–2020) was 0.99 [0.84– 1.10] °C higher than 1850–1900.[8]~~ Global surface temperature ~~was 1.09 [0.95 to 1.20] °C higher in 2011– 2020 than 1850–1900, with larger increases over land (1.59 [1.34 to 1.83] °C) than over the ocean (0.88 [0.68 to 1.01] °C). The estimated increase in~~ global surface temperature ~~since AR5 is principally due to further~~ warming since 2003–2012 ~~(+0.19 [0.16 to 0.22] °C). Additionally, methodological advances and new datasets contributed approximately 0.1°C to the updated estimate of~~ warming ~~in AR6.[10]~~

All this repetition. The toddler scolded by now; toys taken away; behavior corrected. *& yet the coral bleaches. & yet the coral bleaches. & yet the coral bleaches.*

Momaday, we have become disoriented, indeed. All this data. & Earth's ethic? How wrong questions drip from tongues. Erratum. Lose the etymology of words.

A.1.3 ~~The likely range of total~~ human-caused ~~global surface temperature increase from 1850–1900 to 2010–2019[11] is 0.8°C to 1.3°C, with a best estimate of 1.07°C. It is likely that well-mixed GHGs contributed a warming of 1.0°C to 2.0°C, other human drivers (principally aerosols) contributed a cooling of 0.0°C to 0.8°C, natural drivers changed~~ global ~~surface temperature by −0.1°C to 0.1°C, and internal variability changed it by −0.2°C to 0.2°C. It is very likely that well-mixed GHGs were the main driver[12] of tropospheric warming since 1979, and extremely likely that human-caused stratospheric~~ ozone depletion ~~was the main driver of cooling of the lower stratosphere between 1979 and the mid-1990s. {3.3, 6.4, 7.3, Cross-Section Box TS.1, TS.2.3} (Figure SPM.2)~~

Our predictable, what do you call, natural configurations, designs? *Natural how?*

A.1.4 ~~Globally averaged~~ precipitation ~~over land has likely increased since 1950, with a faster rate of~~ increase ~~since the 1980s (medium confidence). It is likely that~~ human influence ~~contributed to the~~ pattern ~~of observed precipitation changes since the mid-20th century, and extremely likely that human influence contributed to the~~ pattern ~~of observed changes in near-surface ocean salinity. Mid-latitude storm tracks have likely shifted poleward in both hemispheres since the 1980s, with marked seasonality in trends (medium confidence). For the Southern Hemisphere, human influence very likely contributed to the poleward shift of the closely related extratropical jet in austral summer. {2.3, 3.3, 8.3, 9.2, TS.2.3, TS.2.4, Box TS.6}~~

Our enaction of the bystander effect on the Earth. Distress calls
of land. *Listen. The soil calls. The air calls. The water calls.*

A.1.5 Human influence ~~is very likely the~~ main driver ~~of the global~~ retreat of glaciers ~~since the 1990s and the~~ decrease in Arctic sea ice ~~area between 1979–1988 and 2010–2019 (about 40% in September and about 10% in March). There has been no significant trend in Antarctic sea ice area from 1979 to 2020 due to regionally opposing trends and large internal variability. Human influence very likely contributed to the decrease in Northern Hemisphere spring snow cover since 1950. It is very likely that human influence has contributed to the observed~~ surface melting of the Greenland Ice Sheet ~~over the past two decades, but there is only limited evidence, with medium agreement, of human influence on the Antarctic Ice Sheet~~ mass loss. {2.3, 3.4, 8.3, 9.3, 9.5, TS.2.5}

Ignore. Ignore. Ignore. *But you are a natural being in a natural world?* Ignore.
Ignore. Ignore. *But you are a natural being in a natural world?* Our nature = erratum.

A.1.6 ~~It is virtually certain that the global upper ocean (0–700 m) has warmed since the 1970s and extremely likely that human influence is the main driver. It is virtually certain that~~ human-caused CO_2 ~~emissions are the main driver of current~~ global acidification of the surface open ocean. ~~There is high confidence that~~ oxygen levels ~~have dropped in many upper ocean regions since the mid-20th century, and medium confidence that human influence contributed to this~~ drop. {2.3, 3.5, 3.6, 5.3, 9.2, TS.2.4}

{ }
{ }
{ }
{ }
{ }
{ }

Erratum in the missing.
Mourn the biodiversity lost.
Mourn the oxygen lost.
Mourn the glaciers lost.
Erratum in the lack

of mourning.

A.1.7 ~~Global mean~~ sea level increase~~d by 0.20 [0.15 to 0.25] m between 1901 and 2018.~~ ~~The average rate of~~ sea level rise ~~was 1.3 [0.6 to 2.1] mm yr−1 between 1901 and 1971,~~ increasing ~~to 1.9 [0.8 to 2.9] mm yr−1 between 1971 and 2006, and further~~ increasing ~~to 3.7 [3.2 to 4.2] mm yr−1 between 2006 and 2018 (high confidence).~~ Human influence ~~was very likely the main driver of these~~ increases ~~since at least 1971. {2.3, 3.5, 9.6, Cross-Chapter Box 9.1, Box TS.4}~~

Errata in the gorging. We do not love ourselves fully, hooks. Estrangement riddles our neurons, our cells, our decisions. A lack of evidence that we honor the Earth. Our bodies in dereliction of the sacred. *Connection never lost, only forgotten.*

A.1.8 ~~Changes in the land biosphere since 1970 are consistent with~~ global warming~~:~~ ~~climate zones have shifted poleward in both hemispheres, and the growing season has~~ ~~on average lengthened by up to two days per decade since the 1950s in the Northern~~ ~~Hemisphere extratropics~~ (high confidence)~~. {2.3, TS.2.6}~~

Confidence of remember.
Confidence of remember.
Confidence of remember.
Confidence of remember.

Confidence of remember.
Confidence of remember.
Confidence of remember.
Confidence of remember.
Confidence of remember.

Triptych of Understanding *Law* as Human-Made Construct with Fundamental & Detrimental Errors

I. Law of Water

The Ohio River snakes the belly of the *So Much to Discover* state. You stand in Cincinnati, face in brisk wind, grip the metal railing lining the church cliff & overlook the water. You think of a nation; a nation possessed by borders, liminal spaces— deny/permeate an argument in our flawed brains. A human kidney is made up of 85% water: the lungs, 80%. You shutter. Stone in your throat, hairs on your neck rise. The article read, *unofficial extension of the Mason-Dixon Line*. Nothing *unofficial* in this place, clouds form a spinal column above your head, dissipate. You think of the Great Migration, of the amygdala's governance on the body. Your jaw rolls *extension* & you chew & chew the physicality of division—north/south, black/white, free/not free—delusions of a country, where a confederate flag becomes a swastika, a badge: a symbol of racial violence. A sickness of bias encodes in our minds: we call this sickness racism; we call this sickness white supremacy. How we haunt ourselves. You feel your own ghost here, in claw & tension behind ribs, between vertebrae. Your ghost whispers to echoes of lives passing through, passing in, the streaming below. Your cells hold ancestry of migration. You came to the water to see; you came to the water to understand your brown body taking space where history unravels it; you came to the water to pray the tension inside & outside your chest subsides, heals. You came to understand we hold inside us both curse & cure; time warp & time; a new testament to tear down borders, laws, policies that abandon the marginalized. How imaginary lines continue to carve wounds in Black & Brown communities. Claudia Rankine said, "because white men can't / police their

imagination / black people are dying." To close your eyes &
imagine a future lineage not scarred with incarceration & death.
To see with your own eyes, the crossing. To see with your own
eyes the crossing should never have been necessary.

II. Law of Numbers

In a system, a

      body   a system, seen
                as system   not seen

calculation in statistics   say *correctional control*   300,000 Ohio residents under
                       say *correctional control*   233,000 people on probation in
                       say *correctional control*   makes our state fourth
in a grotesque accolade   say *correctional control*   of mass correctional control

leaders in   lock up incarceration   separation   cleaving of a life, living.

In a system, a

      Black body   a system, seen
                as system   not seen   3% of Ohio population
                                        34% of jail population
                                        45% of prison population

In algebraic expressions, letters represent variables: numbers
in disguise. In an X+Y equation, understanding begins with C.
Look at C. Calculate back. Some words that begin with C:
corrupt, cops, crowistic, cognitions, create, concocted, criminals.
Now look at R. Calculate back. Some words that begin with R:
racist, rules, regulate, roles, restrict, reformed, radicalization.

All equations carry a weight of history. Solving for whom?

What happens to a broken equation? Who sutures the math? Makes the illogical logical? Who gets to be mathematician? Who number? Over & over, who number? Say *inequitable power distributions* & feel the failure of language, failure of numbers, failure of laws; how systems designed with racists ideations seismically destroy a life in motion, a life living in a system that does not see.

Today	12,600 locked up in pretrial. {people}	Tomorrow 12,600 locked up in pretrial.
Next day	12,600 locked up in pretrial. {people}	Day after 12,600 locked up in pretrial.
Day after	12,600 locked up in pretrial. {people}	Day after 12,600 locked up in pretrial.
Day after	12,600 locked up in pretrial. {people}	Day after 12,600 locked up in pretrial.
Day after	12,600 locked up in pretrial. {people}	Day after 12,600 locked up in pretrial.
Day after	12,600 locked up in pretrial. {people}	Day after 12,600 locked up in pretrial.
Day after	12,600 locked up in pretrial. {people}	Day after 12,600 locked up in pretrial.
Day after	12,600 locked up in pretrial. {people}	Day after 12,600 locked up in pretrial.

We teeter on curve-less lines in spike   & our lips mouth *exponential growth*

& our lips mouth *sister, brother, father, mother, cousin, lover, husband, daughter, son, friend, aunt, uncle, uncle, uncle, uncle*

a plea   before the wrist snaps   we've always known of the wrestling

a litany of human beings—   what division resembles in a body

of flesh   body of state   body of collective thought   body of free{dom}{will} body torn

by a system that breaks us, cracks our spine
& mocks:
now dance;   *you said you wanted to dance.*

III. Law of Cells

We internal as much as external. We, our frontal lobes
in synapse & fire. We, our tissues on bone in govern
of cells. We flesh on tissues in govern of cells. We organs
in govern of cells. Cells of our bodies: cytoplasm
of biomolecules of proteins & nucleic acids enclosed in membrane.

On January 5, 2021, Ohio's inmate population = 43,695

30 trillion cells inside one human body.

July 2020 inmate numbers =

23,544	white men & women
20,450	Black men & women
1,819	*other* men & women

Cells bind us. Cells contain us. Cells in tandem design to function
as a whole—not separate us, not collapse us, not redact us—never
meant to define us. So much life inside a cell.

Ohio demographics =

78.6%	white men & women
12.2%	Black men & women
7.44%	*other* men & women

What does it mean to be Black or "other" in relation to the law in Ohio?

19.64% of population, yet 48.61% of inmates in Ohio.

We want to call a broken thing *unconstitutional.* We want to call
a thing that only benefits some *inequitable.* What words mean
to a family without their 30 trillion cells they call *father*—an empty
exists in labels versus actions. Did you vote for something
broken? Do you know it's broken, or do you believe
my *otherness* makes me deserving of a law that whiteness
does not feel the weight of? Do my cells not equal the same
number as your cells? We must be allowed to count. Count all.

Ohio daily average cost per inmate = $64.45

We, not cells on a spreadsheet not adding up. We, not cells of steel
& brick. Our faces not in silhouette behind bar grillage, mortar of 70
square feet deemed *standard minimum* by American Correctional Association.

When do we learn?

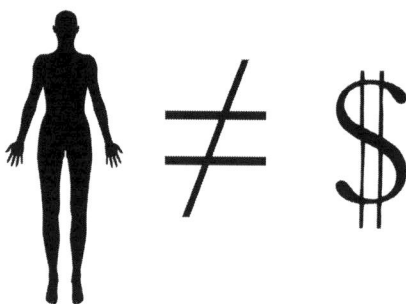

How much does 22,269 x 30 trillion cells weigh? Collapse
in the calculation over the logic. If we must calculate, calculate
only to feel the weight, such immensity of life, contained—
in a system broken by whiteness. Feel the weight in your mind.

Feel.

You might say the system isn't broken; a white system works
for whiteness. Designed by whiteness. No balance ever existed.

We speak of a new type of balance in a postcolonial nation
that has yet to demonstrate equity, what freedom looks like.

Look.

Cells bind us. Cells contain us. Cells in tandem design to function
as a whole—not separate us, not collapse us, not redact us—never
meant to define us. So much life inside a cell.

EXCAVATION

In the Cellular

A Galapagos tortoise's heart beats six times per minute; that's one beat every 10 seconds, or 42 babies born in the world per beat, or the universe expanding 92 miles, or two blinks for the average person, or 1,000 bolts of lightning striking the ground. At a cellular level, the tortoise's body knows its capabilities considering longevity and time. Compare that to the human heart, which beats about 80 beats per minute, or even the hummingbird's heart, which beats up to 1,260 times a minute or as low as 50 beats during torpor. So much can be said about what the body knows and how it prepares for its own existence.

In his essay "Circles," Ralph Waldo Emerson speaks about the soul and its ability to leap over boundaries: "But the heart refuses to be imprisoned; in its first and narrowest pulses, it already tends outward with a vast force, and to immense and innumerable expansions." I'm pondering Emerson's "expansions" and my own heart; the ways in which poetry set up camp behind my ribs and nestled in my aortic sack. Poetry began bodily for me. Poetry found me long before I knew how to articulate it or that my life would be dedicated to it. More on this soon.

***

Let's first consider more fascinations, as fascinations are important. The medulla oblongata functions in delicate regulation of our breathing, our cardiac activity, our sensory neurons, our circulation. Inside the skull, this continuation of spinal cord makes up the lowest part of the brainstem and controls the heart and lungs. Nerve cells travel this superhighway between the forebrain and midbrain. The bulb in the ladder to the cerebellum and cerebrum. All this synapsing taking place under flesh. The interstates of us.

This idea that we are, in many ways, stuck in the interior when it comes to our consciousness, constantly ebbs through my thinking. Emerson said, "The eye is the first circle; the horizon which it forms the second; and throughout nature this primary figure is repeated throughout without end." This connectivity to the horizon and the body has always intrigued me; the role sight plays in our lives is a powerful consideration for how we understand the world and ourselves. I remember the first time I saw the movie *Being John Malkovich.* The strangeness of how humans live through the portholes of ocular bone and cells sent a wave of acknowledgment through me. Our consciousness sits at the helm of a muscular ship as we steer through the physical world. I felt like I was seen for the first time. I turned to my partner and said, "See. See, this is how I feel all the time." The concept of boundaries that Emerson spoke of has always alluded to the interior versus exterior environments for me. I am this mind, but also this body, and with both I am present in this existence. The body as a container, home, vessel for the thinking that is done inside.

> Are you not the sparrow-shadow
> you see above the meadow? How
> the pupil swallows light, for the
> mind to regurgitate pictorially. We
> refract: the lovely art of bending.
> Once you see the sparrow-shadow,
> is it not part of you . . . burnt upon
> the retina; captured inside tissues &
> tendrils of brain? There now,
> witness blueprint & design in
> form.

In all this thinking, my mind drifts to the '80s and '90s when everyone was obsessed with time capsules. Our tiny efforts to collect ourselves in a world that's so much larger than our singular bodies. These were our own contributions to archaeology. The digging in, to one day be dug up. In middle school, I remember obsessing about what to put in my seventh-grade time capsule. Kids had school photos, Bart Simpson dolls, cut braids of hair tied with ribbon, Garbage Pail Kids cards, mood rings, you name it. Thirty years later, I can't remember *what* I put in the capsule, but only the feeling of obsession. What our bodies choose to remember creates paths of understanding for us to later access. What we know about our past is largely what we remember. Beyond cognition, our skin, cells, and muscles also hold their own memory. This memory is at the mercy of what imprints on the cerebellum, amygdala, hippocampus, and prefrontal cortex.

I've always been a personal excavator, a scavenger. As a child, I made forts out of teacup shards, electrical wire the city forgot, broken branches, dirt, and rusted pots left behind the woods just north of the Alden Motel where I grew up. I'd rummage through shoe boxes, cedar chests, drawers, under beds, jewelry boxes, and cabinets when my grandparents left the house. Perhaps my scavenging was the first echo of poetry inside me. No one spoke of history in the Alden Motel. No one spoke of why we stopped speaking Spanish in the house; or why we stood in line at the food bank every week; or why we didn't believe in Santa because the church ladies called us every December to negotiate between our Xmas wishes and their donation budget; or why we gave my mom cards on Mother's Day and Father's Day; or why my sister was put in special ed for being Mexican; or the racial slurs both inside and outside the motel; or the whispers from parishioners; or why the carnations I bought boys on Valentine's Day were always sent back under another boy's shoe. No one spoke of history, our history: Melody, Joe, and me—three brown bodies who weren't allowed to have a history. So, I became an archaeologist of the Alden Motel.

***

Flash back to 1985. My grandparents had left the house for a trip to Penny's in Iowa Falls. I heard the wheels of the Dodge go from gravel to pavement and leaped from the couch. I slunk out of the diner-turned-living room, left at the motel office, past Cindy the biting Pomeranian (but I'd bite too if I were a dog on a leash inside), right at my grandparents' living quarters, toward the blue tarp tacked at the entryway. Grandpa hung the tarp up in winter to avoid heating the two bedrooms up the stairs. "Up the stairs" to this day is still a phrase of dreams for me; it's the place I was not allowed to go; the reliquary of my uncle's muscle car magazines, '70s collared shirts, and my grandma's fake furs. Upstairs was off limits to me, so of course every chance I got, I pulled back the blue tarp.

For years, a door at the end of the hall haunted me. I stood before the door with wide eyes: my own Valley of the Kings. I began to dig and shift the blockade boxes, blankets, and magazines to create a sliver of an opening and wedged my gangly frame inside. The smell of mothballs stung my nose, and I ran my fingers over hanging garments draped in plastic, handles of old vacuum cleaners, and felt hats, until I reached a pile of shoeboxes.

In the Alden Motel, shoeboxes never contained shoes. They held the good stuff: photos, keepsakes, letters, pieces of lace from women I think were related to me. I grabbed the box on the top, stepped back into the light, and sat down in the hallway. Lifting the lid, revealed a conglomerate of photographs. In the hoard of images and faces, one sepia photo stopped me.

In the middle of the square, slightly askew, was a five-foot, two-inch man, tawny skin, thick black mustache, woolen flat cap, and my sister, just a baby, wrapped in his arms. The man held my sister in front of a barbed wire fence with a field beyond. Time stopped. The world lifted a veil, and I could not look away. Entranced, I scoured his face. His eyes were my eyes. His nose bridged and flattened in all the same places as mine. My cheeks were his cheeks. I held my own chin in my hands in the drafty hallway of the Alden Motel and cried. Until that moment, I had not understood replication, genetics, aching, culture, or mourning. All my cells went feral at one time, and my flesh an inadequate boundary. My heart rivaled the hummingbird's pounding, all my internal interstates synapsed and synapsed and synapsed. On one hand, *I came from somewhere* pulsed between my ears, and on the other, *Where is he? Why did he leave? Was I not enough?* bullied their way out as well.

I pocketed the photo. This was the first and only photo I had ever seen of my father.

***

For many years, I was fascinated by the image of this person I had never known. I hid the photo in a sock drawer, then a jewelry box, then in a book. Early on, I took the photo out and each gaze created a gaping hole behind my ribs. At the age of forty, I would finally write the words born inside me the day I found the photo, in a series of poems titled "Dear Coyote."

> I stitch the stars in patterns of your chin, your kneecap,
> your rib, your gait: a constellation of absence. I map
> your body, a celestial cartography to understand my
> own echo, my own cave in the torso, cave of undoing.

In my teenage years, I cursed the photo for my mustache, slanted eyes, my skin.

> witness & your head imitates, back/forth; how
> *brutal* & *bothersome* arrange us; how you, unable
> to look away, lick your lips in disgust of you.

In my twenties, I couldn't look at the photo due to my rage of finding out about the cocaine in the couch cushions, the sex with women while married to my mom, the violence to my siblings and Mom, the radio dedication to "Melody" on her 16th birthday.

> When you beat my brother's face with a sack of potatoes,
> when he bruised & you drew the burlap back for blood,
> did you smell lilac, believe your fists made us into
> something beautiful? When you opened our mother with
> knuckles scented with other vaginas, did you believe in
> your gift, passed? I cup my breasts in the mirror &
> consider the tissues of violence; if I crack my neck, cleave
> at the thyroid & pull out the medulla oblongata, will I
> cross section the parts of you that continue to wound?

The photo is now lost. Lost physically and in the imagination where brain, desires, and cellular history have created a time capsule. This was my first encounter with poetry—in my hands. Poetry seeped up from someplace in my cells, my cognition, my heart, my lungs. It was waiting, waiting for me to be ready. The image of my seven-year-old bloodstream circulating words that would one day become the poetry I needed comforts me. In that photo was a ghost of my face, but I was never his, and he was never mine. He has only ever been a specter lambent across my horizon.

I continue to feel Emerson's words: "I unsettle all things. No facts are sacred to me; none are profane; I simply experience, an endless seeker, with no Past at my back." This is the work of the poet: to unsettle. We first are unsettled by the world that harbors us. We long for a world in which we see ourselves. We long for a world we can look at, full on in the face, without bursting at the seams.

. . . origin

lay only in a compass-less map and the bright bright
burn against the dark {galaxies streaming inside
out} forcing them to *look, look away, look again.*

The past was, and in many ways still is, a mystery to me. We are products of both our genetics and our social constructions. Maybe I saw my snoopiness (as my grandma used to say) as solving a mystery? Aren't we here to discover? From moments of birth, we discover the world in a harsh and challenging way, but unable to fully comprehend what birth means until many years of evolving.

***

Letting go is also an allowance of influence from the artistic process. How can something come from you but never truly be yours? The "not knowing" trancelike state when writing poetry. Letting your obsessions take over can be a frightening endeavor. Poetry, in its unique art form, asks the artist to relinquish some control, to give over to process, for the sake of the art, for *what must be said.* Emerson says, "The way of life is wonderful: it is by abandonment." I believe these words. We must be willing to let go, to release that which contains us, either in the mind or in physicality, to embrace that which we cannot know. This is the risk of creation. In life as in the poetical, it is the moment of letting go that is essential to our true birth: a birth without boundaries, with all the senses open and permeable; a birth into finding comfort in the unknowing; a birth born out of wonder into wonder.

My eye was the first circle. The photo of my father another circle. Our slanting eyes mirrored through genetics, another. The urge to discover, another: a poetry of the body. See how we ripple as natural beings. It was through this gorgeous slanted vision, the part of my body that once disgusted me because it was among the many features that made me *other*, that my poetical existence emerged. Internalized oppression exists in many marginalized people; a colonization of the DNA. I know it does for me. It's how we fight against oppression in the internal and external that matters. My eyes and their slant shape the way I see the world. They are what make me beautiful. A unique gift to have felt violence and still loved. To have been spit in the face and still loved. To have been told I was *worthless, dirty, nothing*, and still loved.

> brain, safe behind skull; think *walls*, think *what*
> *walls keep, what walls inhibit*; how you no
> prisoner & thus, *out out brave other*, into a world
> that throws stones, a world that beats &
> batters; how you, *other*, love bold, love bold.

Poetry begins in the cellular, in one person's cognitions where the impossible becomes possible. I'm a product of impossibility. We all are. The odds of us becoming are not odds one would typically bet on. Every Galapagos tortoise, hummingbird, walking medulla oblongata, found a way here under astronomical conditions. Therefore, poetry cannot happen without our thinking (which Emerson thought was the hardest task in the world). Thinking comes from the brain and the brain is made up of 100 billion neurons and glial cells. I don't know about you, but that fascinates me. Fascinations are important.

We might believe that everything exists without us, and maybe it does, but if a tree falls in the woods . . . well, the woods wouldn't exist without the trees. Poetry cannot exist without us, without our humanity, creativity, imagination, ingenuity, fascinations, cognitions, questioning, risk, and doubt. The doubt of my lineage, of who I was in that hallway in 1985, created a circle of thought that spiraled me into the poet I am today. We are a compilation of motor functions and nonliving organs and tissues that make up a body that lives. We are the epitome of impossible doing the possible. Our bodies have prepared for us. Poetry begins in the cellular.

A SHARP DAWN

Interstitial Archaeology: Make My Mouth a Temple Now, without the Severing of Life or Organ to Unhaunt the Silences Lorde Warns Us About

You run your tongue from palate to velum. A *Smithsonian*
article tells of a gold-foil amulet, tongue-shaped, found in
an Egyptian mummy. You think of the embalmer's thumb
& forefinger lowering the golden replica into jaw, missing
muscle—gap of where the tongue once lay. Careful plot
to ensure speech in the afterlife. To cut out the oblong
shape of organ, landscape of textured papillae, in styloid
process slice making room for elements, Au, atomic
number 79—primordial isotope—in existence from before
formation of Earth. Imagine placing the first star between
molars. How you close any chasm in hold of such wealth-
drawn worlds. How you masticate, posthumously, gaps
from mind to mandible: D**** jumping on your nine-
year-old flesh, yelling, *You're the spic shit pile*, & you weighted
& thin & your maxillary teeth made of mountains, unable
to unhinge the moment A**** admits, *I meant to pay you
$2,000 more, whoops*, how your skin & presence unequal
to her whiteness in her eyes & still you unfurl no sound.
How you masticate, posthumously, these compounding
deaths—all that mouths spin & unspin—from root's
removal from hyoid bone, symbol of dereliction of ideation
in vertebrate anatomy: a cave, rising from mutilation, turned
gift in Taposiris Magna, in cavities becoming temples
from thousands of years buried in sand & then excavation
& you with organ of gold, whisper in heaves: *What atonement?*

Moratorium

Under the breaths of states, a mutter—extend or terminate shut-off protections. & the *Post* article counts the days, 67 of no electricity, no energy, no refrigerator; how the diabetic man stores insulin on ice in a cooler. Disconnections over disconnections. A pandemic ravages us, inside our cells & outside our cells, our gatherings of tissues. Let us count debts in collection from a nation: gas payment, water payment, electric payment. Our economic liturgy. What of the payment of calling a country home? Muscle payment, silence payment, blood payment. A country swears to protect its people. *We hold these truths* . . . & we crave the *self-evident*, we crave the *created equal.* A country lies about protecting its people. Decimation of a declaration. We speak of class in continued whispers & whispers lodge & swell inside the body of our nation, a sore in blister before burst. Dream still in sag, still deferred, Langston. We speak of waves & crashes: second wave of infection, Dow Jones crashing, waive of bills—stop adding us up; we must be beyond statistics to our country. A percentage of a percentage: a life kept in cages of debt, cages of broken structures allowing cops to legally murder without consequence, cages of steel & iron of detention centers along the border, cages of language without empathy on the first lady's lips, where the headline read, "'Give me a fucking break': What Melania Trump said about the blowback against family separations."

An hourglass keeps our humanity in turn, upside down, & turn; we in the belly a collective of sand, afraid of the shatter & fall— how we must break a system to build a new, to form solid architecture to hold our granular bones while still active in flesh. Our dead interments impatient for us & we yell, *Stay back,* we phoenixes burning a future imagine of our wings. To be cinders means the heat exits; the heat exists as breath too, breathing: a rhythm of proof, a rhythm of a body's survival. We rip our joints, our muscles, our throats, our minds from the subjugation of a nation in the business of burying the living.

To Put Meat Back

You stand in pajamas, *haaaw* out your breath
to the sharp morning & count the scarlet
robins in perch of branches—drops of blood
on finger bones—an end, like a synapse
slides into the crevasses of your cells; aren't we
always transmitting in response to impulse
here among the gray atmosphere, trees crack
wood lightning into the gravestone clouds
hide the myth of permanent cessation, secret
to regeneration, what we forget when doused
in infections & over a million lost & moratoriums
& unemployment rivals 1929–1939 & a nation
hesitates to crack its knuckles, to put meat back
on this skeleton before the winter licks us dry.

Hawk Hymn

My knees in loose soil, knuckles in earth. A type
of weathering occurs when we release our bodies
into elements. I hold the bulb & peat in palms. Sacred
exists here in each tendril of root. Sagacity veins each
Lily petal. Above, five hawks loop the air. Five hawks
with scapulars & coverts outstretched; a demonstration
of aerodynamics of lift & drag in my pupils. How ulna
& radius in my wrists transmute to ten wings in swoop.
Whittle us down: skeletons all—mobile in our thin
& hollow bones. Skeletons in defiance. I met Death
once as a rodeo clown, thumbs sliding under suspenders
in whisper to bull before rider devoured in horns. Once,
Death almost drowned: a fly in my chili; sauce-soaked wing
lifted with spoon onto the counter; buzz of a hundred
hordes of locust shook inside a tiny body. I watched
until flight became possible again. I am convinced
we are meant to defy. A long screech renders the quiet
sky with a tapestry of keel-shaped sternums; flight
centers where muscles attach; intersections of tissues
& breastbones make the hawks strong. I raise my hand
to shield the sun; take five steps, ataxia in my limbs
in dizzy of the hawks' infinite circles. Their frames
lower. *Had these been buzzards?* I once felt a buzzard's
talon on the neck of a rabbit. I gasped in the air stolen
from us; a country of gaps went to the streets. Hawks
come now, in tandem, to bear witness to my upturned
chin; my retinas etch their silhouettes for my optic nerve
to carry to my brain & memory & memory: a form
of keeping. These hawks are portents. Passages
of becoming. If a hawk feather be a voice, let me call
up from my throat, *Keep your plumage full & broad. The float*

inside you requires a gathering. I believe the hawks know
we stand at the precipice of conjure. A bellow
of names spoken to transform history, a gathering
of our voices. & those who deal with the lives
of others, shudder at the psalms resounding; shudder
at the feathers no longer theirs to pluck. It is Sunday here.
It is Sunday here & I open a rib for the hymns.

Used to Be

The dead minks in Denmark make me think about language, the way we hide & package in sound bites. 15 million minks killed over COVID-19 infections. *USA Today* uses the words *slaughter* then *cull*, while the article dances with images of furry zombies rising from graves—explained easily by rushed burials & shallow plots—the pandemic rushes & slows time & minds in unfathomable superpower-esque ways these days. *These days.* Another consideration of language. *Unprecedented times.* On social I saw a joke posted: *Could really use some precedented times.* I wanted to laugh. The bridge between want & fruition collapsed for me in June 2020. I'm still hunting for a contractor, magician with the tools to repair a damage I don't fully understand. We used to be *all right*. We used to be *okay*. We used to hug & hold & greet friends with double kisses on cheeks, shake hands, pull babies not ours into our arms the shape of cradles, eat pozole with spittle flying from our tongues in boisterous laughter amid dim lights of a packed restaurant, dance with our heat & sweat pressed to a stranger, lover, one in the same for the night, fuck in back alleys on planes on swaying decks near boat houses, clasp hands in lines to create bodies as roadblocks, bury our dead & weep into shoulders of loved ones with only our mourning & not thoughts of saliva or transmission & we knew what the face of our deceased looked like before burial before cremation & we celebrated the life taken from us too soon too soon. We used to be *all right*. We used to be *okay*. We used to be:

Monster Talk

Your eyes narrow on me. You want me hollow—skin attached only to a scaffold where lungs, liver, thyroid, membranes hide from your look of *You can't possibly know a man's fist?* I tell my cheeks, *Be stable.* I tell my heart, *Suture close. Wounds not allowable here.* & the stale space between our breath elongates across the physical gap between us. I hold very still & think of Evelyn. Grandma Evelyn, who put cold washcloths to my forehead when the light sensitivity hit. She'd hold my chest down with her hand, *Hold still, Felicia. Only still and the ache knows to leave.* Her remedy never fully cured me, yet I learned how exhale transforms a severing mind & here under florescent lights my knees go limp, my torso settles into my abdomen & my eyes meet yours & our tongues silent. All the fists I've known: Fist of my brother with the kitchen knife. My hair braided in fists & the sound of my forehead on concrete. Fists at my jaws. Fists at my sternum. Fists at my back, my skull, my ribs, my pelvis, inside my vagina without consent. Fists with my wrists curled inside them, broken off & somehow still attached to my body. Fists pointed at me before strike, strike, strike. My fists unable when my body ripens in the first morning light. My fingers unable now, to contract at your look—my therapist says I withhold expressions of anger. Fists of José Francisco Senior purpling my mother's flesh; the reasons my brother legally changed his name. Inside a cranium tolls: *Can we map the genetic passing of father's fist to daughter's fist?* Fists tear my sweater's shoulder before heave of my six-year-old frame into the snowbank. The same knuckles turn the steering wheel into a Dairy Queen's parking lot to buy me ice cream before I learned *Chirophobia* means the "fear of hands" & I want *Fūstphobia* from Old German to mean "fear the five in huddle" & yet I dislike my therapist. A history of fists charts—a strange cartography of what my body holds. Now, you see in my retinas your own broken questions, a dereliction of form & we release without words.

Tempest in the Cerebellum

I fell. On a flat sidewalk on a snowless, iceless, sun-streaked afternoon. No impetus of flail: palms, then elbows in catch of concrete, then belly, knees, & pinch of chin in aftershock; a body in sweep of inertia held close to gravity's chest: mother's arms missing my touch. Slow motion in the blink, blink of eyelids processing scene: I lay, blocks from my destination, visible to the lawns, visible to those behind hedges & panes & corneas & lenses & retinas & optic nerves—cerebellum failing, too, momentarily in trance. How we can't think ourselves outside the physical limbs & muscles & organs & flesh that circumvent us through time & space. We are our own riddle's riddle. We, delicacy thrown. What are we: Egg? Or moment of hatch? Shell seconds before crack? Beak inside—*peck, peck, peck*? Comb & wattle: a future maturation? Hen in incubation? Hen in whisper of lay? I lay—a display—mainly a repository amid my own tempest of brain in whir & burrow. I can't remember the seconds on ground, minutes even. I remember seeing foxglove, blooms of bells enticing; how compounds of berries used to treat heart failure—ingestion effects similar to that of unregulated heart medicine. Mind, not unlike the foxglove: three parts beauty on the verge of one part toxicity. I wanted to blame. I wanted to blame the light rail for ten seconds later; I wanted to blame the sidewalk for unevenness, for cracks or shoddy craftsmanship; I wanted to blame the word *craftsmanship* & all patriarchal undertones & why *constantly on guard* cycles & cycles; I wanted to blame the heat, the desert for taking & absorbing my liquid, making my ankles & feet swell; I wanted to blame my dormant clitoris, the lack of orgasms, yearning for a person 500 miles away at the foothills of the Rockies; I wanted to blame the tingling in my throat & chest for being another brown woman as spectacle; I wanted to blame a god, an Old Testament god, for the story of gardens & snakes & ovaries & blood as fault lines & all metaphors of *the fall*; I wanted to blame discoveries of new black holes for not sucking me in & up just bit more; I wanted to blame *discovery* & lack of a brief pause, how only if my attention diverted, how one second behind; how one second behind. I turned over & sat up to a Chihuahua barking five feet from me, squatting as if to pee. I barked back. Just once. We both got up, walked away part bruised, part satisfied.

Mars Exploration: Poem for Diana Trujillo & the Work of Wonder

In the '80s, the term *martian* hit my body with either slurs & fists or cartoony depictions of hungry Alf-esque Muppets or Marvin's neon green. How even in galaxies far far, we can't imagine beyond a masculine invasion. In the 2021 article, Diana Trujillo helps design the rover's robotic arm; Diana Trujillo wonders if we are alone; Diana Trujillo carries the word *director* in her title as she stands in front of the blue, red, and white NASA sign; Diana Trujillo's headline reads, "From Cleaning Lady to Director for NASA, This Latina Immigrant Just Put a Rover on Mars," & I wonder about performance, if the fourth wall crumbles for us or just haunts; I wonder about walls & what a country makes us carry/leave behind; I wonder about documentation, what a country makes us prove beyond ourselves over & over again, a culling reminder if my name shows up in national print, will someone write: Felicia Zamora explores poetry to understand gaps in the world; Felicia Zamora knows alone is a symptom; Felicia Zamora carries the word *migration* in her bones & a university logo in her email signature; Felicia Zamora's headline reads, "From Toilet Bowl Brush to Pen, This Latina Just Wrote Another Book of Poems . . . So What?"; I wonder how years scouring the Dairy Queen toilets in Iowa Falls, or palms sliced in cornfields working underage for the detasseling company my brother nicknamed the *Bloody Cock*, or days standing in line at the food bank with my mother, might surface & define me—in a succinctness meant to make me unaware of myself; I wonder, how far we go in any parody, plunge our hands into any planet's soil before we see ourselves—& wonder what discovery really means.

How Fire Works: A Fourth of July Consideration

We want loud of loud, greens transform
from yellows, swish, twinkle twinkle, the booms
that shake inside the diaphragm—yet we hung
people from our trees. Shadows of bodies haunt
a ground, a land sour from the take. The smell
of carboard & sparkle of sparklers, flash powder,
cordite in burn, a singe in our nostrils—yet we tied
people to bumpers, how gravel 30 miles an hour
on flesh, america knows how to peel you away
if you aren't white, aren't cis, aren't a man,
aren't able-bodied, aren't the labels a country
remains allowed to carve from its people. You know
with kerosene & kitty litter & matchheads you can rig
a firecracker. Or a small capsule of 50 mg of powder
& a fuse. Explosives in our cupboards, our shelves,
our mouths, our wounds. Be terrified
of what we celebrate. The crackle & *one-one*
thousand before the rumble—we count,
america. Tearing down the statues, fists in air
knuckles the color of onyx, umber, tawny
with the knees of the badged on necks in scorch
of our retinas. You know how fire works. All
things ignite under enough chemicals in resistance,
enough pressure, enough—hyoid bone becomes
flint & our bodies in streets, in motion now
& the voices we hear—the voices our own.

Monopoly

The ship. I always wanted the ship. Tight to play
the ship. & that Ol' shoe. Stank. & trust me, Fry's
words—*What smells like boot feet?*—from *Futurama*
scroll through my head, butter on hot corn. & yes
Matt Groening cartoons mythically find ways into
my poems. Don't they yours? I quote *The Simpsons*
intimately like a twelve-year-old '90s boy with his
twelve-year-old friends. Roll the accusations in hurl
at my feminism, or loose feminism, or "bad" to pay
homage to Gay's insurmountable genius. Let me
love on women in this poem; juxtapose embraces
of estrogen right next to Homer, not the epic one,
well, not that kind of epic, that plump & sunflower
icon of my childhood living inside me still. Gay, I
couldn't agree more on how nostalgia fixates inside
the gelatinous curves & creases of the brain.

In the news, the Justice Department files a lawsuit
against Google. The US government, this country,
our governing body with broken judicial systems,
hiring god-complexed politicians to sever basic
human rights from marginalized populations,
claims an unlawful monopoly on Google over—
power. Power over internet searches and, surprise
surprise, internet advertising. Oh, Capitalism, you
barbed-wire heart of this nation, scraping at cells &
flesh & bleeding us from the inside out. Capitalism,
you leak in the hull unable to patch yourself, unable
to scoop the rising water out of your guts so you
toss the life preservers over, pock holes in life rafts
to ensure you don't go down alone. Capitalism, you

tantrum-throwing child with the remote yelling, *Fuck Rose & her comfortable British UN seat. Fuck Jack, for being in poverty* (& how you ignore your hand in socioeconomic class & how you only watch movies with white actors . . . like we don't notice). Are antitrust actions against Google unnecessary, Lemieux? Is internet dominance temporary? Who's keeping whom safe? Golden age of noir & again we piecemeal in black & white. Temporary dominance alludes to the player's ability to mutate the game. Game board pieces circling & revolting. Game of a game—never being asked, a forcing. Thimble, dog, wheelbarrow, top hat, iron: objects. The way a country sees humanity. Who am I kidding? I always knew the ship meant a battleship.

Neuron Fire: Or I Want Brown & Black & Queer Joy to Be Ubiquitous: Or What We're Made of Connects Us, *Fuck*: Or I Am Writing This Poem when I Should Be Out Protesting so This Poem Is a Protest Instead

I wonder about vulnerability. Envisage. How my third metacarpal
smacks into wood & the purples surface skin long before tender
before my eyes package up the scene for nerve cells to detect
in a type of mystery only cells talking solves. I carve a love poem
to my body inside the skull, in hopes all eyes roll back far enough
to read my inscription in shitty penmanship. In maturation outside
the womb, to explain our thinking means a study of brain chemicals,
electric signals, neurons as neighbors—cityscapes under flesh. Our
thoughts propagate in neuron fire. Waves of waves of waves—signals
of us, compounds in coalesce. Peel us back to reveal a galaxy of burning
hydrogen & helium & churn of nuclear forges in our guts; heaven
held in the pin pricks of pin pricks. My body a constellation of elements
of stars gone supernova—transient & astronomical my atoms—stellar
fusion gives me assemblage in a last evolutionary stage before explosion.

The Bird

I leave Kleenexes around the house. *A pandemic thing*, my partner tells me & reminds me of Kleenex-the-brand versus *tissues* as the overarching item. Moments such as these—I give bow & prayer to whoever invented the gesture of the middle finger. *The Bird*, for all you ornithologists. I retract my hands in fold in remembering the Greeks used the middle finger in representation of male genitalia, how Aristophanes's character's finger moves from gesture to crotch in a rhythm only a play titled *The Clouds* in 419 BC gets away with. Then the false 1415 Battle of Agincourt claim, that French soldiers cut off middle & index fingers of captured archers, so the British arrow slinging ceased. All the ways men compare a cock— longbowmen, the lot. Snopes debunked the Agincourt mutilations claim along with the phrase "pluck yew" evolving to "fuck you," which feels clever, even in the falsehood. I begin to wonder about all this myth & origin of story. I want to go back to my Kleenex parade & yet giving my partner the Bird & considering origins feels more pertinent than ever. Consider all the testosterone in our stories. How story sutures in some cultures, cleaves in others. I want to know the study of hands, a da Vinci-esque attention to the middle finger, my middle finger; place where palmistry & chirology meet to read the feminine history of my tallest finger. A fashion blog tells me my middle fingers harbor significance of balance, law, and justice. I raise my Birds high into the air. I consider how any symmetrical person might come up with that conclusion. How do we undo phallic embodiments of cock & balls of the finger to knuckles & find women's power here? Romans named the gesture digitus impudicus—shameless and indecent; I consider all ways society, the nation, the world, label my vagina, my XX chromosomes, as offensive. In the *Epigrammata*, Latin poet

Martial's character extends *the indecent one* to three doctors, first century AD *suck it*—which again, brings in the phallic, sexually explicit & ownership of the gesture by men. Male squirrel monkeys gesture with their penis, Tacitus wrote that German tribes gave the Bird to advancing Roman soldiers, or so says the historian at University of Illinois who writes on the rhetoric of insults, & in all the litany of myth, not one speaks of women. My mind floods with a severing between me & what I thought I knew about my relationship to the Bird. I hold my right hand in my left fingers, rub my middle finger with thumb, pause gently at the callus, *writer's bump*, I whisper to myself. How skin creates a barrier of dead skin cells to protect the underlying skin; what develops in repeated friction, repeated tensions. Crayons to markers to pencils to pens . . . my middle finger & I in a love story crossing time & my body's development. My middle finger understands pressures & speaks for when flesh must—I hold my middle finger out, homage to my writing journey, & tell the history of the Bird, *Go fuck yourself.*

Chris Martin Sings *Shiver* & I Shiver: A Poem for Madam Vice President

This poem isn't for Coldplay or rock 'n' roll or the Honda speakers or the 275
on-ramp to Dayton, OH, on November 11. This poem isn't for Martin. Isn't for the way

his stool shook at First Avenue where I touched his foot, sweaty palmed & sweaty breasted,
before Apple, before Madison Square, & mouthed, *This Coldplay's gonna be big.* This poem

isn't for my grandfather, or his *You'll never amount to anything* gutturals, his *You dirty
spic; waste of sperm* pupils in spit at my brown body, my brown irises. This poem

isn't for the associate provost who pulled me into his office after the 2016 election,
saying, *We liberals will always be disadvantaged, Felicia, because we're unwilling to do horrid things*

to win, after asking me about my undocumented family, after asking, *You're Mexican, right?*
This poem is not for his damaging white liberalism. This poem isn't for the playground

splashed with my blood after being punched in the face by the kid a grade above me & *Fuckin'
Taco* in his saliva. Isn't for the asphalt, the snickers or that kid . . . all those kids.

This poem is for Kamala Harris. Madam Vice President Kamala Harris. This poem
is for my little brown body between my grandfather & the television, alert & still, not running

away, a demand to be seen. This poem is for my moon boots, thrift-store gems, & the tip
of the right boot in that kid's groin. This poem is for my mother, who wrote nine children's

books in the '80s & not one accepted for publication. This poem is for *The Bear That Changes Colors, Glasses for Tommy Tiger, Betty Butterfly's Strange Mirror,* & the author's signature: *Linda*

Zamora. For the reason I became a poet—to write a poem to Madam Vice President—to say the word *possibility* & believe it. This poem is for the trillions of false litanies to women—*You*

can't X. Can't Y. Don't Z. Don't X. Cunt. You should X. You should Y. Fuck off. You don't belong. Don't get your panties in a bunch. Let me mansplain X. Relax. It's just a joke. You wanted this—may

this match burn these all down. This poem is for women. This poem is for women. This poem is for Trans women. This poem is for Queer women. This poem is for Black women. This poem is for Brown

women. This poem is for Truth & Tubman & Parks. This poem is for Dove & hooks & Sanchez. This poem is for Anzaldúa, Baez, Cisneros. This poem is for women. This poem

is for Madam Vice President Kamala Harris. This poem is for how Martin sings *Shiver* & I shiver at your smile the night the electoral votes hit 290 blue. I see my face

in your smile—all the faces of history. I shiver for history. I shiver for my smile inside your smile. I shiver for the necessity of shivering long overdue, shivers of shivers.

This poem is for the ghazal. This poem is a ghazal because it's a world view. We stitch the stars down to earth now. We stitch the stars deep inside the soil of us, cells, salt-water

guts. We stitch with hair & wishbones for eyes, stitch until fingers bleed & then we stitch on top of the stitches. We taught ourselves to sew. We taught ourselves out of invisibility

the difference between the shadow cast & the body & yet part of the body & how a shadow means a body exists, a body in light. Step in, dear sisters. Step in.

ACKNOWLEDGMENTS

Immense gratitude to all my beloveds; without you, none of my writing is possible. Mel, Joe, Foula, Diana, Shi, Mindy, Cathy, TC, Stephanie, Bruce, Beth, Mom, Lauren, Jack, Jess, Renee, Ausma, Paul, Heather, John, SueEllen, S.A., Angela, Tammy, Mark, Wes, Jenn, Katie, Heather, Sharrell, Leah, Jenny, and Joanna—thank you for believing in me, seeing me, and holding space for me. As always, Chris, we spin and spin and spin on this rock, and every turn, quake, and float with you is a gift. Love you.

Thank you to the University of Wisconsin Press and editors, Sean Bishop and Jesse Lee Kercheval, for bringing this book into the world and for working so hard on the book's behalf. Huge thank you to Sheila McMahon on your keen and generous eye on editing this book.

Thank you to the support from the Charles Phelps Taft Research Center at the University of Cincinnati, the Ohio Arts Council Individual Excellence Award team, and the PLAYA Artists' Residency in Summer Lake, OR.

Much appreciation to the editors and publishing teams of the following journals and magazines in which these poems first found literary homes:

AGNI: "Hawk Hymn"
Alaska Quarterly Review: "Chris Martin Sings *Shiver* & I Shiver: A Poem for Madam Vice President," selected for *The Best American Poetry Anthology 2022*
The American Poetry Review: "Meditations on Ghosts"
Black Warrior Review: "Interstitial Archaeology: Make My Mouth a Temple Now, without the Severing of Life or Organ to Unhaunt the Silences Lorde Warns Us About"
Boston Review: Ancestors Project, "Meditation on Lines"
Boston Review online: "Chirality" and "Monster Talk"
Guernica online: "Poem about Human Habits of Consumption That Begins with Contemplating the Walnut in My Yard"

Honey Literary: "Learned Intimacy" and "Mars Exploration: Poem for Diana Trujillo & the Work of Wonder"

The Journal: "Abecedarian for My Estranged Mexican Tongue" and "Used to Be"

The Georgia Review: "Sonnets to Break the Crown of Invisibility" (Weak follows my jaws), "Sonnets to Break the Crown of Invisibility" (*Dear, don't touch*), "Sonnets to Break the Crown of Invisibility" (Environment echoes us), "Sonnets to Break the Crown of Invisibility" (Tides & centrifugal forces), all four published under "A Quadriptych: Sonnets to Break the Crown of Invisibility," winner of the 2022 Loraine Williams Poetry Prize

The Main Review: "Sonnets to Break the Crown of Invisibility" (*Here, I saved this for you*), "Sonnets to Break the Crown of Invisibility" (My body a ghost of an outline), and "Sonnets to Break the Crown of Invisibility" (Shears of season, bleats)

The Missouri Review: "Sonnets to Break the Crown of Invisibility" (Mind astray), "Sonnets to Break the Crown of Invisibility" (What turns to glass?), and "Tautology of Phrases, Tautology of Mathematical Logic in a Time of Climate Crisis"

New South: "The Bird"

Nimrod International Journal: "Sonnets to Break the Crown of Invisibility" (Sound a bell)

Ninth Letter: "Sonnets to Break the Crown of Invisibility" (Thoughts in cerebrum, brainstem, cerebellum:)

Pleiades: "Ghazal Containing My Estranged Mexican Tongue"

Poetry International: "Moratorium," winner of the Cavafy Poetry Prize

Poetry Magazine: "Lilacs" and "Meditations on Flesh"

Poetry Northwest: "Exhume"

Portland Review: "Tempest in the Cerebellum"

Smartish Pace: "Monopoly" and "To Put Meat Back"

SWWIM, Sing the Body Anthology: "Neuron Fire: Or I Want Brown & Black & Queer Joy to Be Ubiquitous: Or What We're Made of Connects Us, *Fuck*: Or I Am Writing This Poem when I Should Be Out Protesting so This Poem Is a Protest Instead"

Texas Review: "To Haunt Air: In Consideration of Longing, the Potoo, Desire, Gallstones, & What We Remain Still For" and "Taut Logic of Crisis"</LIST>

A version of the lyric essay "In the Cellular" was published in the anthology *The Encounter: A Handbook of Poetic Practice* (Parlor Press, 2022). Many thanks to the editors at Parlor Press who continue to support my writing.

In December 2020, I was one of sixteen artists selected from cross-disciplines in art to win an Ohio Pre-trail and Racial Justice Grant funded by the national Art for Justice Fund to commission a triptych poem on racial justice in incarceration in Ohio, titled "Triptych of Understanding Law as a Human-Made Construct with Fundamental & Detrimental Errors." The poem is part of a larger visual installation, accompanied by a voice recording of the triptych, available as part of *Artful Souls + Liberated Voices: A Virtual Exhibition Featuring Ohio Artists for Pretrial Justice.*

"Tautology of Phrases, Tautology of Mathematical Logic in a Time of Climate Crisis" and "Taut Logic of Crisis" are part of *No One Saves the Earth from Us but Us*, a collaborative song-cycle project on environmental justice and climate change.

NOTES

EPIGRAPHS

James Baldwin, "James Baldwin & Nikki Giovanni Part 1," *Soul!*, WNET Group, 1971.
Evie Shockley, "what does it mean to be human?," in *Suddenly We* © 2023 by Evie
Shockley. Published by Wesleyan University Press. Used by permission. Christopher
Soto, excerpt from "Then A Hammer // Realized Its Life Purpose," in *Diaries of a
Terrorist*. Copyright © 2022 by Christopher Soto. Reprinted with the permission of The
Permissions Company, LLC on behalf of Copper Canyon Press, coppercanyonpress.org.

"MEDITATIONS ON LINES"

Amiri Baraka, "Expressive Language," in *Home: Social Essays*, published by William
Morrow & Company, Inc. Copyright © 1963 by Amiri Baraka. Reprinted by permission
of Chris Calhoun Agency.

"CHIRALITY"

The phrase "how I am more than a casualty" is in direct conversation with the quote
"I am not only a casualty," from Audre Lorde's "The Transformation of Silence
into Language and Action," in *Sister Outsider*, © 1984, 2007 by Audre Lorde. The
phrase "a razor white background" is in direct conversation with the phrase "a sharp
white background," from Claudia Rankine, excerpts from *Citizen: An American
Lyric*. Copyright © 2014 by Claudia Rankine. Reprinted with the permission of The
Permissions Company, LLC on behalf of Graywolf Press, graywolfpress.org.

"MEDITATIONS ON GHOSTS"

All epistolary to Gloria is in conversation with Gloria Anzaldúa and the essay "Speaking
in Tongues: A Letter to 3rd World Women Writers."

"SONNETS TO BREAK THE CROWN OF INVISIBILITY"

|||||||||||||: The word "animality" is used in thinking on Vanessa Angélica Villarreal's
"Interview on the Failure and Violence of Language and Western Consciousness,
Colonial Borders Internal and External, Animal Consciousness," Poetry as

Radicalization & Liberation for BIPOC & Marginalized People Conversation Series, June 2, 2021, https://www.youtube.com/watch?v=ZXIddWBTwsI.

||||||||||||: Poem in conversation with Zakiyyah Iman Jackson, "On Becoming Human: An Introduction," in *Becoming Human: Matter and Meaning in an Antiblack World* (NYU Press, 2020), 39 ("holds the potential to transform"), 33 ("humanist prize"); and Vanessa Angélica Villarreal, "Interview on the Failure and Violence of Language and Western Consciousness, Colonial Borders Internal and External, Animal Consciousness." Much gratitude for all the thinking and inspiration these two scholars and writers have given me.

"TAUTOLOGY OF PHRASES, TAUTOLOGY OF MATHEMATICAL LOGIC IN A TIME OF CLIMATE CRISIS"

Equations for electricity and natural gas: Lindsay Wilson, "Calculate Your Carbon Footprint," Shrink That Foot, accessed May 2021, http://shrinkthatfootprint.com/calculate-your-carbon-footprint. This poem is also in conversation with the following articles: Damien Cave, "Great Barrier Reef Is Bleaching Again. It's Getting More Widespread," *New York Times*, April 6, 2020; Kim Stanley Robinson, "Kim Stanley Robinson on Cities as a Climate Survival Mechanism," Bloomberg, April 17, 2021, https://www.bloomberg.com/news/articles/2021-04-17/the-city-as-a-survival-mechanism-kim-stanley-robinson; "Global Greenhouse Gas Overview," United States EPA, accessed May 2021, https://www.epa.gov/ghgemissions/global-greenhouse-gas-emissions-data; Randy Miller, "1, 2, 3, 4, 5, 6, 7: Plastics Recycling by the Numbers," Miller Recycling Corporation, February 10, 2019, https://millerrecycling.com/plastics-recycling-numbers/.

"ERRATA"

Poem in conversation with sections A–A.1.8 of Intergovernmental Panel on Climate Change, "Summary for Policymakers," in *Climate Change 2021: The Physical Science Basis* (Cambridge University Press, 2023), 1–2; N. Scott Momaday, "An Ethic of the Earth," in *Moral Ground: Ethical Action for a Planet in Peril*, edited by Kathleen Dean Moore and Michael P. Nelson (Trinity University Press, 2011); and bell hooks, "Touching the Earth," in Moore and Nelson, *Moral Ground*.

"TRIPTYCH OF UNDERSTANDING *LAW* AS A HUMAN-MADE CONSTRUCT WITH FUNDAMENTAL & DETRIMENTAL ERRORS"

Section I: "because white men can't": Claudia Rankine, "July 29–August 18, 2014 / Making Room: Script for Public Fiction at Hammer Museum," in *Citizen: An American Lyric*, 135. Copyright © 2014 by Claudia Rankine. Reprinted with the permission of The Permissions Company, LLC on behalf of Graywolf Press, graywolfpress.org.

Section III: inmate population, January 5, 2021: Department of Rehabilitation and Correction Population Count Sheets, https://drc.ohio.gov/Portals/0/1063.pdf; inmate numbers, July 2020: Ohio Department of Rehabilitation & Correction, "2020 Annual Report," https://drc.ohio.gov/about/resource/reports/annual-reports/annual-report-2020; Ohio demographics: Data USA: Ohio, accessed January 2021, https://datausa.io/profile/geo/ohio; Ohio daily average cost per inmate: House Bill 439 of the 132nd General Assembly Fiscal Note & Local Impact Statement, Ohio Legislative Service Commission, March 20, 2018.

"IN THE CELLULAR"

Ralph Waldo Emerson, "Circles," in *Essays by Ralph Waldo Emerson* (1841), 218–35; "Are you not the sparrow-shadow?": Felicia Zamora, "& wings made of matchsticks," in *Of Form & Gather* (University of Notre Dame Press, 2017); Felicia Zamora, "Dear Coyote," *Boston Review*, June 28, 2019, reprinted in *I Always Carry My Bones* (University of Iowa Press, 2021); "witness & your head imitates": Felicia Zamora, "Watching Breed," in *Instrument of Gaps* (Slope Editions, 2018); "When you beat my brother's face": Zamora, "Dear Coyote"; Emerson, "Circles"; "origin / lay only in a compass-less map": Felicia Zamora, "Broken Things," in *& in Open, Marvel* (Parlor Press, 2018); Emerson, "Circles"; "brain, safe behind skull": Felicia Zamora, "Love Bold," in *Body of Render* (Red Hen Press, 2020).

"MORATORIUM"

This poem is in conversation with the first line of the Declaration of Independence to ask whose truths, which self, which evidence, whose equality. The headline is from Nicole Narea, "'Give Me a Fucking Break': What Melania Trump Said about the Blowback against Family Separations," Vox, October 2, 2020, https://www.vox.com/policy-and-politics/2020/10/2/21498660/melania-trump-immigrant-family-separations-recording.

FELICIA ZAMORA is the author of six books of poetry, including *Quotient* (2022); *I Always Carry My Bones* (2021), winner of the 2020 Iowa Poetry Prize and the 2022 Ohioana Book Award in Poetry; *Body of Render* (2020), Benjamin Saltman Award winner; and *Of Form & Gather* (2017), Andrés Montoya Poetry Prize winner. She won the 2022 Loraine Williams Poetry Prize from *The Georgia Review*, a 2022 Tin House Next Book Residency, and a 2024 and 2022 Ohio Arts Council Individual Excellence Award. Her poems appear or are forthcoming in Academy of American Poets *Poem-A-Day*, *AGNI*, *Alaska Quarterly Review*, *The American Poetry Review*, *The Best American Poetry 2022*, *Boston Review*, *Ecotone*, *The Georgia Review*, *Guernica*, *Gulf Coast*, *The Iowa Review*, *The Kenyon Review*, *The Missouri Review*, *Orion*, *Poetry Magazine*, *The Nation*, *West Branch*, and others. She is an associate professor of poetry at the University of Cincinnati and a poetry editor for the *Colorado Review*.

WISCONSIN POETRY SERIES

Sean Bishop and Jesse Lee Kercheval, series editors

Ronald Wallace, founding series editor

How the End First Showed (B) • D. M. Aderibigbe

New Jersey (B) • Betsy Andrews

Salt (B) • Renée Ashley

(At) Wrist (B) • Tacey M. Atsitty

Horizon Note (B) • Robin Behn

What Sex Is Death? (T) • Dario Bellezza, selected and translated by Peter Covino

About Crows (FP) • Craig Blais

Mrs. Dumpty (FP) • Chana Bloch

Rich Wife (4L) • Emily Bludworth de Barrios

Shopping, or The End of Time (FP) • Emily Bludworth de Barrios

The Declarable Future (4L) • Jennifer Boyden

The Mouths of Grazing Things (B) • Jennifer Boyden

Help Is on the Way (4L) • John Brehm

No Day at the Beach • John Brehm

Sea of Faith (B) • John Brehm

Reunion (FP) • Fleda Brown

Brief Landing on the Earth's Surface (B) • Juanita Brunk

Ejo: Poems, Rwanda, 1991–1994 (FP) • Derick Burleson

Grace Engine • Joshua Burton

The Roof of the Whale Poems (T) • Juan Calzadilla, translated by Katherine M. Hedeen and Olivia Lott

Jagged with Love (B) • Susanna Childress

Salvage • Hedgie Choi

Almost Nothing to Be Scared Of (4L) • David Clewell

The Low End of Higher Things • David Clewell

Now We're Getting Somewhere (FP) • David Clewell

(B) = Winner of the Brittingham Prize in Poetry
(FP) = Winner of the Felix Pollak Prize in Poetry
(4L) = Winner of the Four Lakes Prize in Poetry
(T) = Winner of the Wisconsin Prize for Poetry in Translation

Taken Somehow by Surprise (4L) • David Clewell

Thunderhead • Emily Rose Cole

Borrowed Dress (FP) • Cathy Colman

Host • Lisa Fay Coutley

Dear Terror, Dear Splendor • Melissa Crowe

Places/Everyone (B) • Jim Daniels

Show and Tell • Jim Daniels

Darkroom (B) • Jazzy Danziger

And Her Soul Out of Nothing (B) • Olena Kalytiak Davis

Afterlife (FP) • Michael Dhyne

My Favorite Tyrants (B) • Joanne Diaz

Midwhistle • Dante Di Stefano

Talking to Strangers (B) • Patricia Dobler

Alien Miss • Carlina Duan

The Golden Coin (4L) • Alan Feldman

Immortality (4L) • Alan Feldman

A Sail to Great Island (FP) • Alan Feldman

Psalms • Julia Fiedorczuk, translated by Bill Johnston

The Word We Used for It (B) • Max Garland

A Field Guide to the Heavens (B) • Frank X. Gaspar

The Royal Baker's Daughter (FP) • Barbara Goldberg

Fractures (FP) • Carlos Andrés Gómez

Gloss • Rebecca Hazelton

Funny (FP) • Jennifer Michael Hecht

Queen in Blue • Ambalila Hemsell

How to Kill a Goat & Other Monsters • Saúl Hernández

The Legend of Light (FP) • Bob Hicok

Sweet Ruin (B) • Tony Hoagland

Partially Excited States (FP) • Charles Hood

Ripe (FP) • Roy Jacobstein

Last Seen (FP) • Jacqueline Jones LaMon

Perigee (B) • Diane Kerr

American Parables (B) • Daniel Khalastchi

The Story of Your Obstinate Survival • Daniel Khalastchi